About the author

Kingsley L. Dennis, PhD, is a s
He is the author of several crit............ ....ng
New Consciousness for a New World, New Revolutions for a Small Planet, After the Car, and the celebrated *Dawn of the Akashic Age* (with Ervin László). He previously worked in the Sociology Department at Lancaster University, UK, and was Research Associate at the Centre for Mobilities Research (CeMoRe) at Lancaster University. Kingsley is the author of numerous articles on social futures; technology and new media; communications; global affairs; and conscious evolution. As well as academic training, Kingsley has also lived and worked for many years overseas, and travels widely. He currently lives in Andalusia, Spain. Kingsley can be contacted via his personal website: www.kingsleydennis.com.

To ANNA,

A BOOK FOR A PHOENIX
GIRL! ENJOY...

WITH LOVE,

KINGSLEY

(ARCOS, AUGUST 2nd, 2015)

Also by Kingsley L. Dennis

THE PHOENIX GENERATION

A New Era of Connection, Compassion and Consciousness

KINGSLEY L. DENNIS

WATKINS PUBLISHING
LONDON

Dedication

To those of the Phoenix Generation
For knowing *who* you are & *what* you have to do.

To the Women of the World
For being nurturers, and for showing us the values
we need as a collective humanity. For being mothers,
carers, and for helping the world to be a better place.

To my MUM
Who brought me into the world, nurtured me, and
who thinks everything I do is (in her words) *brilliant*!

This edition first published in the UK and USA 2014 by
Watkins Publishing Limited
PO Box 883
Oxford, OX1 9PL
UK
A member of Osprey Group

For enquiries in the USA and Canada:
Osprey Publishing
PO Box 3985
New York, NY 10185-3985
Tel: (001) 212 753 4402
Email: info@ospreypublishing.com

1 3 5 7 9 10 8 6 4 2

Edited and typeset by Donald Sommerville
Printed and bound in Great Britain

A CIP record for this book is available from the British Library

ISBN: 978-1-78028-792-8

Watkins Publishing is supporting the Woodland Trust, the UK's
leading woodland conservation charity, by funding tree-planting
initiatives and woodland maintenance.

www.watkinspublishing.co.uk

Contents

A Note from the Author

The young people whom I refer to as being part of the Phoenix Generation may not even read this book – or be reading printed books at all! Yet although this book is *about them* it is really a book *for us*. It is a book concerned with understanding what is to come and also the potentials that may create the future. It is likely to be a future without any historical precedent. As I explain, the transition toward a world inhabited by the Phoenix Generation is going to be one of those 'flat Earth to round Earth' moments. When it does arrive, we are likely to think 'but how could it have been otherwise!' This transition over the coming decades – and into what I term the *quantum renaissance* – is not going to happen with a 'Big Bang' event but rather with an organic unfolding. For us, we will see new generations arising into the world who will step up to become the architects of a new planetary society. In the grander evolutionary scale of things, all this will occur as if a sudden flowering, or late bloom. Yet we have to realize that for human beings to evolve through change we need to *normalize* and *assimilate* the new anomalies into a balanced perspective and worldview.

So this book is for us – right now – at this precise moment. It is a 'transition tool' to enable us to work with and assist the changes confronting us and human society in general. It is a book to help us recognize the new ways and new models that are most likely to emerge over the coming decades. It is a book to allow us to recognize that many old forms and structures are no longer conducive to a balanced and sustainable life and that we have to let them go. It is a book that affirms a new perspective on the world and how we need to integrate this into our lives without fear, apprehension or distrust. And importantly, it is a book about recognizing the hearts, minds and souls of the new beings entering our human species. So when we look into their bright, enquiring faces we can say to them – 'Yes, we *get it* too . . . and we get you!'

Then, when the sun rises on a new dawn, we can all say we witnessed the glorious new phoenix arising from the ashes . . . and *it was good*.

Kingsley L. Dennis
La Casa Roja
Andalusia

Introduction

What We Do Next Is Important

Dear reader, traditional human power structures and their reign of darkness are about to be rendered obsolete.

Buckminster Fuller

Dear reader, let me expand upon the above opening quote by adding that this obsolescence of the old will usher in the unexpected, the unprecedented, and the spectacularly new. I am not talking about a period of rejuvenation, as this suggests a renovation of the incumbent systems. I am speaking in terms of new forms, new arrangements, new structures, new perspectives and new emerging states of *being*. It is about time we stopped talking about the 'end of things',[1] and instead focus our energies upon creating and fulfilling our positive, potential futures.

Those readers familiar with my work will know that I have repeatedly stressed that a new paradigm is upon us. Also, that how willing, open and receptive we are to these new models, systems and values will determine how the years ahead play out for us – individually and collectively. We are, quite literally, shifting from one set of

C-Values: Competition–Conflict–Control–Censorship – to a new set: Connection–Communication–Consciousness–Compassion. This shift in value systems is being initiated through a confluence of energies that are emerging through people and entering into the world, as this book discusses.

In our physical structures we are reaching critical tipping points – transitional moments – in our social systems, resource systems, financial systems, and in the Earth's environmental systems. On a personal level, we are being critically tested also in our worldviews, values, perceptions and sense of meaning and well-being. All these issues I have discussed in my previous books.[2] Whilst many voices have been harbingers of collapse, I have attempted to emphasize that instead of a disintegration of our global systems we are going through a 'Renaissance of Replacement'. What I mean by this is that rather than entering into a conflict with existing systems through protest and revolution (the old model), we are now engaging in *revolutionizing* our old systems and models through gradually replacing them with emerging innovations and creative new models. And this new renaissance is not emerging from the centre – where the incumbent power structures are strongest – but instead is rising from the periphery. This gradual form of replacement (or takeover) is actually a better model for social transition. One reason is that it avoids a head-on conflict with existing power structures – it *out-does* the old rather than *out-fights* the old. Secondly, it is a more psychologically balanced process as it allows time for people to adapt to the changing social environment – and this is an important concept.

In historical and sociological studies the focus is largely on external data – the laws, institutions, rites, customs, economy and so on – while the psychological aspects of humanity are often neglected. The mental, emotional and spiritual elements associated with the human being have been considered as lesser elements within our social history. Our studies of societies have often suffered from a lack of in-depth psychological understanding. Just as we have social evolution so too must we recognize how this impacts the *psycho-spiritual* state of humanity; we also need to recognize how this impacts and integrates into our human use of technologies. By referring to the psycho-spiritual state of humanity I am suggesting the psychological and the intuitive aspect, as well as the general well-being and inner states. In this book I indicate that as a planetary species we are shifting from the rationalist–individualist era to a psycho-spiritual era that is integrated: a species in unity (not uniformity!) that is also diverse, local and yet globally orientated. Without such foresight and conscious awareness we may witness the continuation of incumbent systems deteriorating into mechanical repetition. That is a way of life devoid of real meaning and maintained by force of custom, attachment and a sense of false security. The fixed idea in the end becomes the enemy of innovation. The extreme manifestation of this is when social order merges into a form of irrational authority. A social order that does not recognize the need for relevance, harmony and fair balance loses touch with its source and turns into a crystallized parody of itself. This is the 'grisly elf' that the Indian philosopher Aurobindo writes of:

> [Man] harbours within him a grisly elf
> Enamoured of sorrow and sin
> The grey Elf shudders from heaven's Flame
> And from all things glad and pure;
> Only by pleasure and passion and pain
> His drama can endure
>
> Aurobindo, *A God's Labour*, 5: 99

The 'grisly elf' within us perpetuates our sorrow and often offers great resistance to the change of power, as if wishing to hold back the tidal forces of transition. Perhaps for too long we have been relying on cleverness without cultivating sufficient wisdom. Perhaps our drawback has been that we were attempting to solve problems without first addressing our very perceptions, perspectives, and patterns of thinking. With the goalposts shifting, so must the game – and the players.

I am convinced that the world will come together in countless ways – with innovative changes in our communication and our uses of technology, through conscious awareness, through people-centred action, and more. These emerging and unfolding events are simply too numerous to list completely or follow. These are the seeds coming to harvest as part of a re-awakening, re-ordering, and re-balancing on this planet. We should recognize that the issues at stake are much larger than governments – they are global and dispersed throughout the peoples of the world. These issues are also too important to be left in the hands of governments alone. We, the people, now need to implement the new ideas coming to the fore. If we are only able to conceive of those ideas that belong to the limits of our thinking then we will do ourselves a great disservice. The future will be about seeing beyond our limitations – thinking anew, and in ways we are currently unaccustomed to. This is the new consciousness – not conceiving or perceiving within the old patterns. We must be ready and prepared not only to catalyze others into awareness and action but also, more importantly, to catalyze ourselves!

External change is not enough if there is no real change within each one of us. If we lack internal understanding, coherence and balance, then it is more difficult for us to reach out and connect to others in tolerance and fairness. We must be ready to shrug off our chains of cultural conditioning[3] and to resist the 'fear of freedom' that has seeped into our social lives as a structure of obedience to manipulated, and often false, norms. Empowerment must become internalized, and yet in harmony with our external lives and responsibilities.

We also need to be prepared to make changes; and to make a difference. We need to be willing to bring positive joy, meaning, and compassion for one another into our lives; to do things for others; and to spread the uplifting human energy. A person cannot invent their state, or artificially construct it: it must come through a genuine and honest presence. As the Persian poet Jalal ad-Din Rumi, known in the West simply as Rumi, says, 'Either exist as you are or be as you look.' If one truly wishes to help the world, we can begin by being ourselves what we wish others to be – and to transform the world by sincere example. Again, quoting Rumi, 'Let the beauty we love be what we do.'

For these reasons I have devoted a majority of Part One of this book to examining the psychological, emotional and inner states of the human being as we move through the transition years ahead. The current generations will be the ones who will have to shoulder the mental and emotional responsibility of change as they are forced to let go of both external and internal systems and states that are no longer beneficial to our future development. This is why I have termed our current generation as the 'Bridge Generation', as it will be required of us to straddle between both worlds. Those generations that come after us will be born *as change* rather than being born *into change* – this is a slight yet very significant difference.

Further, things may appear to be taking a step back before they are able to shift forward: this is the reaction of the old energy. The old energy will struggle and, in many cases, die hard. It will create a collective groundswell of fear, anxiety and insecurity as it sees its old seat of power slowly dissolving as a new quantum renaissance emerges. This new renaissance of connection, communication, consciousness and compassion will rise to usher in an era where the notion of nonlocal connectivity, energetic fields and diversity within unity will become the norm. The chapters in Part One – Building the Bridge thus discuss how the Bridge Generation must be grounded and balanced to work with the disruptive changes in society. In order to 'build the bridge' that will help steer us through the years ahead we will need not only to shift our perspectives but also to change the old system game-play by silently overwhelming the incumbent models – to make the new age the *new normal*.

Part Two – New Mind Rising examines how humanity is benefiting, and self-developing, from its extended connectivity and communication networks. In other words, I discuss how humanity is hard-wired to adapt physically in response to emerging global networks of connection and collaboration. The three chapters in this section discuss how people interact with new technologies; the impacts of social media; new emerging youth groups; and the rise of a global empathic mind. The influences of new social patterns of connectivity are giving rise to an increased planetary empathic awareness. The power of energetically-connected individuals is fuelling the 'We' feeling and bringing the disenchanted together to develop their networks. I also talk about how we are witnessing the increasing rise of the maverick tinkerers, innovators and creative minds. This rising of new models is pushing against the old, self-centred and vertical control systems. Such new systems are showing that a new type of mind is arising, which will mark the generations to come.

Part Three offers an over-arching perspective on what I refer to as the Phoenix Generation: those children being born now who will be young adults around 2030. It is suggested that it will be this generation that will work toward forming a planetary society -- a transition more radical than the shift from agrarian to urban life during the Industrial Revolution. This is a revolutionary transition from national–cultural consciousness to global awareness and planetary consciousness. What this entails is not only a structural shift but also a qualitative one, a shift in our values, psychology and consciousness. Part Three also discusses how those of the Phoenix Generation will be born with increased instinctive intelligence and with a greater degree of inherited wisdom. In these chapters I talk about how at birth the human quantum field calibrates with the Earth energy and how a different state of energy will affect the DNA of the baby and its growth. I also explore how a quantum renaissance will emerge based on the latest findings of science coupled with increased instinctual intelligence. This new era will give rise to changes in many diverse areas of social life, such as health, well-being, politics, media, technology use and cosmic awareness.

In the final chapter I discuss the unfolding recognition that other realities exist beyond the confines of our three-dimensional material reality. There are not only inner worlds and outer worlds – there are also *other* worlds that occupy a zone we are touching upon yet unfamiliar with. I talk of the existence of multi-dimensional realities where space and time as we know them are seen as constructs coming from a linear reality and materially based mindset. It is not that our current 'reality' is breaking apart; it is more the case that other energy realities are breaking through – thus requiring us to reconfigure and recalibrate how we perceive and interpret our constructions of reality.

The recognition that we are part of a living, dynamic universe within resplendent multiverses – teeming with life within multi-dimensional realities – will gradually emerge as the new perspective and worldview for humankind. A new epoch in the evolutionary development of humanity will have begun.

The hypothesis I put forward in this book is that, in accordance with evolutionary trends, a new form of consciousness is unfolding on this planet as new generations arrive. This new wave of consciousness will gradually seep into the core of all our future societies. It is my view that there is no alternative to the evolution of consciousness.

Our responsibility now is to engage fully and be a part of the human *becoming* that we truly wish to see in the world. This requires that we spearhead the energies and models of change for those of us now and, more importantly, for those to come – and this shall be our true legacy.

Welcome to the future – it's going to last a long time . . .

part one

BUILDING THE BRIDGE

Part One examines how those of us who are aware today are required to assist in the transitioning world. The four chapters in this section discuss how the Bridge Generation must be grounded and balanced to work with the disruptive changes in society. In order to 'build the bridge' that will help steer us through the years ahead we will need not only to shift our perspectives but also to change the old-system game-play by silently overwhelming the incumbent models – to make the new age the *new normal*. Such workers are referred to as the 'New Monastics'.

Chapter 1

The Way We Have Lived

'There is no wisdom where there is no common sense.'
Ancient saying

Things are seriously shifting, and have been for some time now. We don't need to be rocket scientists to understand this; nor do we need to be psychics to sense this or 'sensitives' to feel this. Our own innate sense of being human is recognizing, and responding to, a life increasingly out of balance. The 21st century began with confusion: a mixture of millennial optimism with insecurity and ambiguity. The urge to *think forward, move forward*, was sandwiched between new strategies of aggression and violence that were deployed to create social fears and global injustices. The first decade of the 21st century stumbled along without any clear conscious focus, only to fall into a financial quagmire in 2008.

Now, as we prepare to acclimatize to the second decade onwards of the new millennium, we are faced with bankrupt nations, insolvent cities, and disintegrating infrastructures. Our educational systems are failing our children, and either sapping their brains or chemically zapping their neurons. Almost all of us know that something is seriously amiss with modern human life. We feel it instinctively, yet we have been left hanging, indecisive, not knowing how to respond to these issues. There is both external and internal angst accumulating within the mass of humanity. There are blockages, leakages, bursts and explosions appearing both within our social world as well as in Nature. Gaia – our planetary home – is showing us that *movements* are under way, some of them not conducive to current modes of human life. Humanity itself appears to be collectively frustrated and out of patience. This is the way we have lived, and it nurtures us no more.

Our shortcomings include our perception of scarcity. With an abundant spirit, within a world of abundance and giving, we focus our attention onto the scare of scarcity, and perpetuate the abasement of poverty. The rampant inequalities in many of our so-called 'civilized' societies perpetuate the divisions that pull us apart. Our 'old mind', a remnant of an era of industrial growth amid imperial designs, moulded – or rather conditioned – a collective agenda around the pursuit of material self-interest. Conspicuous consumption – an often frantic and unnecessary consumerism – was promoted as the bastion of 'freedom-loving' individuals. We were oblivious to the fact that affluence was linked to inequality.

We have also perhaps forgotten that true richness resides with our well-being. The more privileged in our modern societies have been cultivating private spaces, a process that alienates the less privileged, which in turn creates a lack of trust and increased social division. We have been rendered unaware of the creeping private control of public spaces. This especially concerns the Internet, the newest public venue, which is now the latest battleground between transparent public space and regulated privatized space.

Politicians and those of old-mind 'newspeak' refer to our social inequalities and absurdities as 'sobering'. Why is it that those with vested interests speak as if modern life has made us intoxicated? Do they know something that is not yet public information? We are now faced with a great need – that of making a shift into a new meaningful era. We need to move beyond stale thinking, unhelpful categorizations, and outmoded and increasingly irrelevant ideologies. The current cultural values of civilization have created planetary illness and have manifested dis-ease.

The unnatural state of the human condition which we see in aspects of our social and cultural systems is not our genuine innate human self but a polluted, unbalanced self. We have become accustomed to illogical systems of living and often heartless self-gratification, instead of being supporters of humane rationality and empathy. We have been conditioned to accept disparity and inequality, which serve as triggers for the need to fight our way to the top. Modern society taught us to better ourselves over our neighbours, as long as we don't get any grand ideas about upward social mobility. The mob of celebrity admirers are fuelled and fed by glossy glamour and sparkly sex-gossip that creates a grand distraction. Rather than excelling ourselves by standing on the shoulders of giants, we have often disgraced our-selves by sleeping on the backs of pygmies.

The natural order seeks rebalancing – and so too must we. Yet it is imperative that we are mindful of how this instinctive need for coherence is addressed within a world all too eager to foster the illusion of well-being. We are witness to a world that is awash with grand announcements of spiritual rebirth, guru-ism and self-help commercialism that forms a smooth and slick veneer of good feelings. If we are not careful, or considerate enough, many emerging aspirations are in danger of being lost in a cultural fog of blandness, or, worse, deceit. The deluding greed for short-cuts, for prescription enlightenment, and for supply-on-demand answers has percolated into the globalization model of modern culture. We have personages masquerading as modern-day prophets, and platitudes parading as pro-fundities. Within this cacophony of soundbites – of 'shock and awe' – we have perhaps lost a sense of the innate human self.

Many of us have been distracted, or sidelined, into indifference. We have been told we lack the power to make any lasting change. We have been fed on dis-empowerment whilst evolutionary change, imperceptible to most of us, has been operating on many levels to remodel the playing field. Waking up to the absurdity of the situation has taken time. In the meantime the planet has been divided through ideologies that have been exploited as specific tools of separation. Ideologies either ran amok or were pushed and forcefully propagated around the world as imperial slogans. Media coverage of the early years of the 21st century largely centred on insecurity, so that unease and fear were paraded like mascots by opportunistic governments. This insecurity was often deliberately directed toward a fear of change in order to strengthen incumbent structures of authority. Ongoing and impending systemic breakdown has been interpreted by the mainstream as catastrophic rather than catalytic. Yet now the parameters of understanding and perception are shifting.

Why? Because human consciousness is undergoing a shift – the collective consciousness of humanity is becoming more aware of itself. This emerging wave of awareness is seeping through diverse individuals first, energetically inspiring and catalyzing others. And this change of conscious awareness is set to develop and spread much faster. This is why the decade ahead will be a testing time as it marks the peak clash between two paradigms – or rather two defining eras.

A Clash of Paradigms

The outgoing era is the one which has largely defined the recent century and a half of unprecedented growth and technological advancement and discovery. The model for this era consisted of the industrial extraction of fossil fuels, constructing superhighways of concrete, installing heavy cables, developing global trade zones, centralizing business into mega-corporations and so on. It was an era defined by heavy industry and machinery and was marked by high energy use. Yet it was necessary

17

in forming and developing our diverse societies into a planetary body of interconnections. However, it is now apparent that the countless systems we have come to rely upon are in a state of vulnerable criticality. Current and upcoming years are thus set to play out a series of sharp, short-term hazards that are economic, environmental, geopolitical, societal and technological. As nation-states contend with the old model of requiring increasing amounts of energy and materials to sustain economic growth there will be an escalation in the struggle for control of resources. This will result in a realignment of political relationships throughout the world. It is fair to say that, for the first time, we have entered a phase of civilization in which issues of planetary survival now outweigh more traditional issues of international conflict.

Over the previous centuries there have been successive global power shifts, as indicated by the rise and fall of empires. Yet in recent history there has occurred a higher frequency of such changes, which signals an acceleration in the redistribution of global power. Prior to the twentieth century, global preeminence by a leading state generally lasted for a century or so. Yet, within the recent decades, we have witnessed an incredible level of flux in the power-play upon this planet. We should not underestimate the covert manoeuvring set to take place upon the world stage over the next decade or so. There appears now to be an increasing pattern of dispersal in global power. Emerging world powers include such countries as China, Brazil, India, Indonesia, South Africa and Russia. These increasingly influential players are vying for a more integral role in the management of global affairs. Not only are they impacting and changing the 'global commons', but they are also disseminating various ideologies and ideals about modern life and future-building.

Yet this will not be the main playing field where the paradigms will clash, as a new and significant phenomenon is coming into play. For most of our recorded political history, the mass of humanity has lived in relatively compartmentalized isolation. Now, in sharp contrast, we are witnessing the worldwide emergence of the conscious awakening of populations that, until recently, were only sporadically politically active – or often repressed. The widespread global upheaval that will mark the current decade involves financial instability and irregularity; increasing global unemployment; political crises; social unrest and instability; and rising intolerance and frustration from a politically awakened humanity. This period of great transition will also see significant changes in the international balance of power that has the potential to stir up competition among the emerging regional powers. Due to the emergence of such new regional players we are unlikely to see a future dominated by one single state or empire. The days of a single state or fanatic seeking world domination are relegated to Hollywood. People are waking up, and the grand chessboard has new players.

These new players – whether from Western, Middle Eastern, or East Asian regions – are connected with the world to a degree their predecessors were not. Through both physical contacts – such as through education/ study abroad, frequent travel, work relationships, and much else – and through virtual networks – global communications (Internet, mobile phone), social networks, and more – the world is now almost everywhere politically awakened. Today physical distance is being made irrelevant by instantaneous global communications. Both nation-states and their peoples are becoming increasingly interdependent. Millions of individuals are now awakening, and stirring restlessly in pursuit of a better future. The next decade or two will see how the old-mind model of control, conflict, competition and censorship, will contend with the rising new-mind paradigm of consciousness, collaboration and compassion.

In the short term we may find that the political response is to try to arrange the world into more regulated hierarchical structures, driven by nationalistic security fears. We are also likely to find that the incumbent model not only proves too slow to adapt to changing needs but also very reluctant. Conditions may thus become unstable for a while as the world passes through this testing period. This is why, as Part One of the book explains, it is important that people keep their heads whilst others around them are losing theirs. Our current global civilization is witnessing what happens when the trends of increasing complexity, growth, and finally overshoot[1] occur. We are heading into a decade when we will have to re-arrange the very way we think and do business. This is the clash of paradigms – the narratives we live by – and is necessary whereby 'crises' can act to catalyze real and lasting change. Furthermore, new models rarely come into existence smoothly – a change of guard involves disruption as the norm.

The discontinuity of the coming years will require of us that we re-evaluate our understanding of social, economic and environmental interdependencies and needs. Shifting to a new-mind model is fundamentally a question of how to implement a future that benefits the majority in a sustainable and equitable way. As I discuss later in the book, we are likely to see our current heavily centralized systems and infrastructures give way to new patterns of finer, more intuitive, decentralized and distributed networks that foster and empower greater collective participation.

In this remodelling we will become more globally connected through our collaborative communications whilst at the same time developing deeper ties with our own communities. It is imperative that we move into an era of open planetary dialogue as information and communications become even more democratized, accessible and widely shared. As we move through the coming years, and further away from the older paradigm, there will be incontrovertible signs of new patterns emerging that blend more localized ways of living with increased planetary awareness and unity consciousness.

Toward a Planetary Society

We have now entered upon a new phase of socio-cultural and personal evolution. We have arrived at the cusp of a planetary society. Ours is the first human civilization to reach a point where we have the means to connect ourselves as a global society. Yet to do so with success it is imperative we move forward in balance and respect, realizing that true unity comes through coherent diversity. Throughout the successive civilizations of the past 12,000 years there was little or no perception or concern about the genuine considerations and require-ments of a planetary society. The only traces of this were shown in the zeal to conquer and create great empires.

Through the coalescence of city-states into nation-states the need for adequate resources became paramount to continued growth. The First Industrial Revolution that began in Great Britain (1750–1850) revolutionized social, cultural and economic conditions by shifting from the energy resource of wood to coal. Human connection likewise shifted from letter sending to the then rapid telegraph. The Second Industrial Revolution (1850–1920) marked another shift of energy resource from coal to oil, and the production of electricity. Human connectivity in this phase shifted from the telegraph (with cables) to the radio (wireless), and brought the peoples of the world even closer together. Now we are in the midst of a Third Industrial Revolution. Yet instead of referring to this transition as an 'industrial' one I would prefer to describe this profound shift as a Revolution in Human Being – or rather as a *Revolution in Human Becoming*. We are at a stage now where we have the resources and potential to grow up – both as a species and as a civilization. The possibility of a genuine planetary civilization – through diversity in unity – and with the participation of an awakened and aware humanity, was never on the cards . . . until now.

The shift of consciousness set to spread across the planet will impel and empower us, individually and collectively, to be more connected, communicative and consciously aware of our integral relationship with the natural world. This will be the birth of a new narrative for the next stage of human civilization. Historic change beckons.

First, however, we need to break through the limits of our perception by changing our internal narratives.

Chapter 2

Saying Goodbye to Old Mythologies

'A sign is enough for the alert, but a thousand counsels are not enough for the negligent.'
   Ancient saying

In the years ahead we are going to see great change sweeping through our diverse human societies. It will be change not only brought about by intentional minds and willing hearts, but also by necessity, by coercion and from an evolutionary imperative. The 21st century will be equivalent to the dramatic 'flat Earth to round Earth' shift that was thrust upon humanity centuries before. Yet with great social shifts also come paradigm changes in human perceptions and thinking patterns. This is because significant change permanently alters the way we view our role in life, as well as how we perceive our structures of 'reality'.

Yet it is difficult to have a vision of the future if we base our thinking solely around current trends. The upcoming decades are more likely to be based around potentials rather than linear trends and forecasts. One limiting aspect of our current situation is the lack of vocabulary we have to describe these 'potentials', since our human vocabulary is mostly structured towards describing what *is* and what *can be,* rather than that which *could be* beyond our current frames of reference. This illustrates one of the fundamental issues we now generally face: a lack of vocabulary and vision – irrespective of culture – to comprehend beyond our current models. What our modern mindset often ends up doing is projecting, or rather extending, from present 'knowns', since we often lack the tools to conceptualize the 'unknowns'. It can be far too tempting to fall back onto the familiar, the known and the comfortable. The end result is a projection that is an expanded/extended version of current models rather than a new model. The *extended-view* model is thus a continuation upon current models that are themselves based upon, or are appropriated forms of, more ancient patterns of thinking· If we wish for real human development during these critical years ahead then we must leave behind our old-model comfort-zones. We must be prepared not only to think 'out-of-the-box' but rather 'without-a-box'.

Furthermore, in dealing with present incumbent systems our genuine response should not be one of anger, protest or conflict, as these typical old-mind responses will be playing directly into the hands of the very systems we oppose. The new way of doing things is through a non-conflict yet innovative path-building direction. Rather than entering into conflict with existing systems we need to engage in gradually replacing them with emerging innovations and creative new models. This gradual form of replacement (or takeover) is actually a better model for social transition. It avoids a head-on conflict with existing power structures – it *out-does* the old rather than *out-fights* the old.

This is an extraordinary passage of change we are living through, whereby what we do in the years ahead, will create the template for the future. How we are able to perceive and act upon the emerging changes will depend very much upon the patterns of human consciousness: that is, our dominant mythologies. Many of our current ways of thinking lack the ability to discern the uncertain, the unpredictable and the unexpected. Yet it is likely that the future will show different dynamics of development, not linear but rather through states of flux where new, often unexpected, arrangements come into being. However, since the 'modern' human mindset has a bias for dealing with linear patterns and perspectives, there is the danger that establishment thinkers will perceive and/or conceive of a future that is likely to be an altered or adapted variation upon the current model. That is why, I feel, real change will be seen emerging from the periphery rather than the centre, from emerging 'new thinkers' rather than from establishment figures. Also, such emerging thinkers will be from the younger generations to come, manifesting innate new patterns of thinking. In the meantime we of the present generation need to do our work in saying goodbye to the old mythologies, if we are to serve as the bridge generation.

Previous shifts in 'cultural mythology-narrative' have

occurred at various important stages in human socio-cultural evolution. I feel the times ahead are similarly of deep significance to us all and will provide a shift in perspective that will not only influence our physical socio-cultural evolution but the conscious future of humanity. It is likely we are reaching a milestone marking a great change in how we view the way ahead as a collective species.

The present era with its push for corporate global-ization – for international structures of power, regulation and knowledge-control – is but the latest world system that is being pressed upon the majority of minds by the actions of the influential few. Below are other sets of mythologies, as put forth by cultural historian William Irwin Thompson, which help us grasp the nature of perspective:

Analogy One:
Imagine insects with a life span of two weeks, and then imagine further that they are trying to build up a science about the nature of time and history. Clearly, they cannot build a model on the basis of a few days in summer. So let us endow them with a language and a culture through which they can pass on their knowledge to future generations. Summer passes, then autumn; finally it is winter. The winter insects are a whole new breed, and they perfect a new and revolutionary science on the basis of the 'hard facts' of their perceptions of snow. As for the myths and legends of summer: certainly the intelligent insects are not going to believe the superstitions of their primitive ancestors.

Analogy Two:

Imagine a vehicle as large as a planet that began a voyage an aeon ago. After generations of voyaging, the mechanics lose all sense of who they are and where they are going. They begin to grow unhappy with their condition and say that the notion that they are on a journey in an enormous vehicle is a myth put forth by the ruling class to disguise its oppression of the mechanical class. There is a revolution and the captain is killed. Elated by their triumph, the mechanics proclaim the dictatorship of the proletariat and destroy the captain's log, which contains, they claim, nothing but the lies of the old ruling class.

Analogy Three:

Imagine that you have just discovered a civilization as small as a DNA molecule. You want to establish contact, but since your dimensions prevent you from entering the same space-time envelope, you must search for other means of communication. From observing the civilization closely, you find that there is an informational class that seems to carry messages back and forth among parts of the society, and you observe further that these messengers are actually enzymes of a structure that is isomorphic to one of your own patterns of information. Since you cannot talk directly to the members of the civilization, you decide to talk through a patterning of the bits of information the enzymes carry back and forth. Unfortunately, the very act of trying to pattern an enzyme alters its structure so that a part of your own message is always shifted. It seems that the only time the enzymes are able to carry a high proportion of your own message is when their civilizational structure is either breaking apart or just about to come together again. Fascinated by the problem, you choose your opening and closing epochs carefully and begin to carry on an extended conversation with the civilization.[1]

We may wish to consider carefully the type of mythologies we choose to live by. We can possibly see a correspondence between this process and Walter Miller Jr's acclaimed novel *A Canticle for Leibowitz*. The book begins at a time 600 years after a global nuclear war has destroyed 20th-century civilization. In the aftermath, those who survived were vehemently opposed to the 'modern culture' of knowledge and technology which they consider to have been responsible for the weaponry and war. Irradiated tribal mutants, wandering survivors and a few communities and religious institutions (abbeys) remain scattered over the wasteland. One day a monk retrieves, with the help of a wandering beggar, an old scrap of paper which proves to be the remains of a blueprint from a 20th-century engineer. The text is delivered to a local abbey where it becomes venerated as sacred and is copied, worshipped, blessed by the then Pope and exalted to the status of divine relic. The engineer (Leibowitz) is canonized, and the new mythology becomes the guiding manuscript. Finally, one of the monks manages to make a dynamo from

Leibowitz's blueprint . . . skip 600 years into the future and the abbey has been completely modernized during The Age of Light, and space has been colonized. Yet soon war breaks out again, despite the religious guidance of St Leibowitz, patron saint of electricians.

What can be gained from this insightful story is that, in any age, institutionalized mythology might very well be perpetuated by outworn dogmas that are no longer understood and no longer of any developmental value. Also, if old ideas maintain a fossilized religious/spiritual impulse, alongside an overly materialistic, technological civilization, then the consequences for humanity are potentially disastrous and destructive.

In order to shift toward a more positive paradigm – one that is more appropriate for our planetary future – we need to move beyond the pull of contrary impulses. We require a sense of responsibility to establish a developmental path towards betterment ('progress') alongside a collective feeling of incompleteness and unconscious longing ('the fall'). As the cultural historian Richard Tarnas reminds us:

> What individuals and psychologists have long been doing has now become the collective responsibility of our culture: to make the unconscious conscious. And for a civilization, to a crucial extent, history is the great unconscious – history not so much as the external chronology of political and military milestones, but as the interior history of a civilization: that unfolding drama evidenced in a culture's evolving cosmology, its philosophy

and science, its religious consciousness, its art, its myths.[2]

It is the interior history that maps out our potential futures – an internal drama that shifts amongst the myths, cosmology and religious/spiritual impulses. Human life on planet Earth now finds itself within a psycho-physical transmutation, physically adapting to a changing world whilst simultaneously adopting new ideas that correspond to our developmental needs·

Mythologies are collections of stories that we tell ourselves to explain the world and our place in it. Our perspective – the way we think – has been based on a long heritage, or concoction, of such stories. In other words, we are our *own myth*. And the old-mind mythology that we have been living within for so long strives to promote those perspectives that best serve to maintain a status quo of dependence upon authority structures – what can be called the 'scarcity model'. As Richard Heinberg notes:

> As civilization has provided more and more for us, it's made us more and more infantile, so that we are less and less able to think for ourselves, less and less able to provide for ourselves, and this makes us more like a herd – we develop more of a herd mentality – where we take our cues from the people around us, the authority figures around us.[3]

This 'infantile/herd mentality' that Heinberg refers to is an aspect of the old mythology that we need to break away from. A new mythology – what can be referred to as the 'abundance model' – recognizes that abundance does not necessarily imply only material quantity, but that it also reflects an abundance of spirit, vision, creativity, intention and empowerment. This perspective celebrates the fact that we are now living in an inherently interconnected world. Diverse minds around the world are connecting and seeing problems and issues in new ways. Innovation is a state of mind made exponential by our connectivity. We have to change the global conversation from complaining about problems to solving them. We have to be a part of the growing global conversation.

Seeking the Subtlety

In a data-rich world we are in danger of becoming increasingly meaning-poor. Those times when we may experience an elevated, ecstatic or euphoric state of interconnectedness and wholeness have been termed by psychologists as 'peak experiences'. Unfortunately, the potential for engaging intimately with the world has chiefly been replaced by a conditioning that comes with strict cultural parameters and consensus thinking. It is little wonder that there are people who indulge in adrenalin-rich extremes – sport, intoxication, brutality, risk-taking – in order to gain a lost sense of vibrancy and aliveness. There is the danger that many of our modern cultures cultivate a taste – or rather need – for cruder impacts, as if finer experiences are not enough. There is an analogy here in the short tale of the two small boys who were discussing their sweets:

'I wonder' said the first, 'why it is that we always buy the jaw-breaking candy, when that soft stuff is so much sweeter?'

'I buy it because I like to KNOW that I'm eating something!'[4]

It is frequently the finer impacts – the more subtle experiences – which have the greater developmental potential. Nowadays it is often only through experiencing such 'euphoric' moments that we come to realize that our lives are so much more interesting and interconnected than we credit. Unfortunately, many of these epiphanies come from shocks, such as health issues or a tragic sense of loss. It is essential that those of us participating consciously in this bridging generation feel nourished by the finer contacts rather than the cruder impacts offered by the old mythologies (aka propaganda).

We only have to turn on the television and watch the mainstream news to become disheartened by the way the world is going. If we 'believe' this type of news then we likely question if there is any hope on the horizon. As an ancient Eastern saying goes, 'If you insist on buying poor food, you must be prepared to dislike it at the serving.' This could also be paraphrased as, 'If you insist on listening to mainstream propaganda, you must be prepared to receive a bad aftertaste.' We often have to dig deeper to find the uplifting, positive stories: of people coming together despite their warring nations at loggerheads; of people dedicating their lives in service to others in order to make a difference; of old enemies forgiving and forgetting, and forging a new life. We need to recognize that at this time we are all living in a world undergoing transition.

Perhaps we may be having doubts about our own role in these uncertain times. As we increasingly witness so many of the negative aspects of the world it will be ever easier for us to lose our focus, often without realizing it. The creep of negativity can be imperceptible at first. Negative energy thus acts to disturb harmonious and developmental states and to discourage us. There is an apocryphal tale that highlights this:

> Once the word spread that the Devil was pulling out of his business and was arranging to sell off all the tools of his trade to the highest bidder. On the night of the sale all the tools were arranged for the bidders to view. What a motley selection it was! There were sinister tools of hatred, jealousy, envy, malice and treachery, plus all the other elements of evil. Yet, beside these, there also was an instrument that seemed harmless, a wedge-shaped implement that appeared worn out, shabby, and yet was priced so much higher than all others. Someone asked the Devil what was the name of such a poor-looking instrument.
>
> 'Discouragement,' answered the Devil.
>
> 'And why *is* the price so high for such an un-malicious sounding instrument?' asked the bidder.
>
> 'Because', said the Devil, 'this instrument is more useful to me than any other. I can enter the consciousness of a human being when all other ways fail me and once inside through the discouragement of that person I can do whatever I

please. The instrument is worn out because I use it almost everywhere and as very few people know about this I can continue to achieve my goals successfully.'

And as the price of discouragement was so very, very high, even today this tool remains the property of the Devil.

This analogy is fitting for how despondency and doubt operate. We feel that they are overwhelming, when in fact this is their weakness. The truth is that no matter our state of bitterness, anger, frustration or depression, it can be overcome by only the slightest presence of positive focus.

It is understandable that during these years of transition those who are part of the Bridge Generation may feel frustration when it appears that real change is emerging too slowly within a world that paradoxically appears to be speeding up. On one hand the world around us is shifting fast; yet the real change we wish to see in our lives is arriving too slowly for some of us. It can be like the sensation of running in a dream – our mind is running, or telling us to run, whilst our legs are moving in slow motion. The sensation of change, and of passing time, is rapid; but the physical reality of change requires real work at ground level. Yet we have the potential for real and lasting change – let me illustrate this with the analogy of a 'colour revolution'. Imagine a sheet of blotting paper, with our actions as ink drops. One drop of ink on the blotting paper does almost nothing; nor do two drops or three drops of ink. But over time these ink drops gradually begin to spread, and join up, and then we have an 'aha' moment when we suddenly realize that all the drops of ink have merged and the blotting paper is now another colour – the colour of the new 'ink-thinking'. We are those drops of new colour ink. We are each doing our own thing, our personal actions, and yet contributing to the whole. Change is coming, and it has the potential to quietly overwhelm.

Our responsibility during this Bridge Generation is to be ambassadors for the change we wish to see. This means not being afraid of what 'consensus society' may say about our perspectives. We are living through an era in which we are called upon to be responsible for bringing these new models of thought, behaviour and integrity to the world. It will be important to speak our own under-standing – not only to share where we are each at, but also to validate and give strength to our self, family, friends and community. In order not to sell ourselves short it is important we normalize the new mythology. If we become sucked into conspiracy – into paranoid or angry behaviour – then we do a disservice to our ideals and give our detractors excuses to use against us. In our everyday life we are the 'door-to-door salespeople' for the ideals and change we represent and wish to see in the world. After all, we wouldn't buy any products from a frantic, frenetic and frustrated salesperson – would we? So in order to overwhelm quietly the current models/ mythologies we need to become the best we can be, and to normalize the future into being. We are no longer dealing with alternative theories. We are representing the 'New Normal' – not the 'New Age'.

Those individuals and groups aware and consciously awake during these times should be searching for resources for development and empowerment, such as reaching out for like-minded individuals and groups, organizing support networks, and strengthening a sense of purpose, meaning and value. And then, of course, going out and meeting with new connections and communities whenever and wherever possible. In order to be a part of the crucible of change that is in-forming the years ahead many of us will need to awaken from our passive slumber and to grab hold of a new sense of reality.

Yet the change will not occur overnight. We will need to live, experience and respond to the challenges ahead in order to bring forth new solutions and new ways of being and behaving. In other words, we need to change the rules of the game.

Chapter 3

Changing the Game Play

Seek wisdom while you have the strength, or you may lose strength without gaining wisdom.
Ancient saying

There is a story that is told about a wandering stranger who once stopped a king in the street. Furious, the king shouted, 'How dare you, a man of little worth, interrupt the progress of your sovereign?' The stranger answered: 'Can you truly be a sovereign if you cannot even fill my begging bowl?' And he held out his bowl to the king. In wishing to show his generosity to the crowd that had now assembled, the king ordered that the stranger's begging bowl be filled with gold. But no sooner did the bowl appear to be full of gold coins than they disappeared and the bowl seemed empty once again. Sack after sack of gold coins was brought, and still the begging bowl devoured them all. 'Stop,' screamed the king, 'This trick of yours is emptying my treasury!' 'Perhaps to you I am emptying your treasury,' said the stranger, 'but to others I am merely illustrating a truth.' 'And what truth is this?' asked the king. 'The truth is that the bowl is the desires of humankind, and the gold is what humanity is given. There is no end to humanity's capacity to devour, without being in any way changed. See, the bowl has eaten nearly all your wealth, but it is still an empty piece of carved old wood, which has not partaken of the nature of gold in any respect.'

What this tale illustrates is that many of our old ways of doing things are devouring both the world and our own sense of worth, without producing real change within us. Observing our current epoch, with its varied ideological and political conflict, mental conditioning and strife among peoples and nations, it appears that our collective body is in a state of global psychosis. Nothing short of a global revelatory experience, or epiphany, is required.

For the past several thousand years at least the human race has defined itself through crisis and calamity, struggle and greed. We have recently crammed ourselves into conurbations – densely-packed city spaces where daily we pass thousands of people, with tens of thousands more living within a few minutes' travel of where we are, and yet we each act independently, unaware of our intrinsic interdependence. Psychologically we are separated, feeling alone, whilst our inherent connectedness lies under our skin and all around us. In a play by Luigi Pirandello – *The Man with a Flower in his Mouth* – a man emerges from a doctor's surgery with a fatal diagnosis; with this knowledge of impending death the man's world suddenly changes and every small thing has significance. He undergoes a conversion of consciousness: the bleak diagnosis and shock are followed by a courageous renewal. Perhaps ours is a world with a flower in its mouth . . . as we move through the transition and its associated initiatory impacts. Maybe we are facing an historic episode of rebalancing on an epic scale, signalled by spiralling unrest in the collective consciousness of humanity. That we have no cultural memory of having encountered such an epochal transition before places us in frightening new territory. As Richard Tarnas says:

> Perhaps we, as a civilization and a species, are undergoing a rite of passage of the most epochal and profound kind, acted out on the stage of history with, as it were, the cosmos itself as the tribal matrix of the initiatory drama.[1]

Any society or civilization which makes the material world its sole pursuit and object of concern cannot but decline in the long run. That is why the game play needs to change, and why the current generations have a responsibility to be a part of this constructive change.

For us to evolve as a species and as a planetary civilization we need to co-exist with the Earth's systems and to understand those laws that are in harmony with a long-term future. This may be the only way toward advancing the evolution of the human being; and it is common sense too. The famous British historian Arnold Toynbee claimed that civilizations emerge and evolve when they are governed by a creative minority that inspires the people. In turn, civilizations enter decline when the dominant minority fails to inspire the rest of its people and prefers to follow a status quo of power rule. This begs the question – are we being inspired? Or rather, can we be inspired to become the very social agents of change?

Social agents of change are those people in every society who are not afraid to break away from the norms of social conditioning and to think for themselves. The awakened individual is now required more than ever, so that conscious thinking and conscious behaviour can co-create a way forward, through the morass that surrounds us. As I discuss in Part Two, the rising change has already begun – and we need to take notice of this shifting ground.

The bottom line is that we need to accept that there is the possibility for self-development – work on ourselves – that in turn has an impact upon the grander developmental cycle of civilization. We need to recognize that we often live our lives within a distracting social milieu, and how it is crucial we align ourselves with those positive ideas that reflect our capacities and strengths. In other words, to feel empowered and not powerless, to possess an inner confidence that allows us to work in our external environments in the ways most appropriate. It is time to stop playing *their* funny games, and to begin taking responsibility for our own minds and actions. It is time to become the new wave of change agents upon the planet – to facilitate the rise of what I call the new monastics.

The New Monastics

There is an old folk tale which tells of the wise fool who arrives at the door of the king's castle asking for entry. He is immediately told by the guard that the king's decree is for each person to state their business and that anyone who tells a lie has to be hanged. Now, when asked why he has come, the wise fool replies, 'I am going to be hanged.' 'I don't believe you!' exclaims the guard, 'You are lying.' 'Very well, then. If I have told a lie, hang me!' 'But if I hang you,' replies the guard, 'then you would have told the truth and I shouldn't have hanged you!' 'Exactly,' replies the wise fool, 'This is your definition of truth.'

The nature of 'truth' in our subjective world lies more in the realm of rhetoric than it does in relation to any objective sense of the word. Nobel laureate Doris Lessing makes a parody of this in her novel *The Sentimental Agents in the Volyen Empire*, where one of the main protagonists falls victim to the dreaded disease of 'Rhetoric'. In a bid to cure him another friend introduces him to what is tactfully disguised as the 'Institute for Historical Research', when in reality it was constructed as the 'Hospital for Rhetorical Diseases'. Rhetoric then, for Lessing, is a disease that can afflict people almost unknowingly – the disease of misapplied language for an explicit agenda. I wonder if many of us are not also suffering from the disease of Rhetoric? Is it not, after all, the 'rhetorical disease' that has created much of our old-paradigm thinking? It is important that our new models of thinking do not become hijacked and appropriated into a modern mental theme park of political deception, corporate duplicity, Armageddon fears, ET salvation and star-gazing apathy.

Unfortunately for us the 'modern mental theme park' already appears to be in full swing. However, if we look around carefully we will see that life at the centre of this theme park does not look so rosy either. The ride is changing – these are the years when the 'central core' will find itself increasingly vulnerable to the periphery. The incumbent consolidated structures of control are seeing disruptive change emerging in places where they never expected it. These unexpected emergent disruptions – what we can call disruptive innovation – are creating the new wave of change and innovation (as I discuss in Part Two). Rather than having a grand and sudden collapse, what we are likely to see are 'transformational patterns' in which fragments of the old-paradigm cultures persist alongside the emergence of the new ones. That is, the new models/patterns/mythologies will emerge as supplementary ones that will develop parallel with the older models until finally replacing them – the new game rules! Call it a takeover if you will. I prefer to think of it as a transition, with different accompanying levels of smoothness (from quite smooth/fairly peachy to a bit rough).

Another caveat is that within these transformational patterns are also the windows of opportunity for the soothsayers, false prophets, gurus and self-appointed 'spiritual teachers' to take advantage of the increased sense of dislocation and fluidity. We need to be alert to the old minds of the status quo co-opting the new initiatives by incorporating them as their own. This could serve to give the illusion that serious changes are under way. The truth, unfortunately, is that there is little change possible from the core stance of the status quo – our platitudes become theirs, and the only thing that changes hands are empty words. That is why change must be actual rather than theoretical.

As is known from the pattern of social cycles, real change occurs when anomalies – another word for the change agents – become too numerous to be absorbed into the incumbent system. That is why individuals and groups 'doing their own thing' are so important right now. Almost all great ideas and innovations began life as 'disruptive' from the periphery, from 'outsiders' – those people just going it alone, often 'outside the box'. I'd like to refer to such people as the New Monastics – from the monastic model of action whereby individuals/groups just get on and create new ways of doing things without fanfare or large billboard announcements. Such monastic work, so to speak, often operates below the radar, being authentic in activity rather than seeking visibility. The monastic worker, in seeking change, chooses a way of life that has meaning and that can be a heritage for the family and for the future. Often the monastic workers strive to assist change within their own communities. They are like ink dots on the paper, slowly spreading their impact by diligent yet creative work. What makes this model not only more appealing today, but also much more effective, is the rise of global communications and distributed networks. Now, the hard-working monastics can connect, share and collaborate.

We do not need to be waiting around for the 'Next Big Thing' or some grand televised miracle. If we are waiting for the current global system to implode completely before we decide to do something, we might miss the boat. World systems don't disappear – they restructure. This restructuring usually occurs during the decline phase, with parts of the old model struggling on until they become the materials (or spare parts) from which the restructuring emerges. It's not a simple case of one model suddenly coming in to replace another. During the 'rise and fall' pattern there occurs the recycling and re-use of social structures, practices and resources. In other words, the transformation usually occurs within the dynamics of internal collapse. It is difficult at times to see this as transformation, as transition may be indistinguishable from disintegration in the early stages. Yet in times of transition, such as we are in now, the monastic workers have greater potential to effect change because there is so much instability in the world. The 'larger system' is currently more vulnerable to shifts from within. By each one of us making a change, and participating through small-scale contributions, we can create greater impact in the world than we would normally.

It is an ideal time now to look toward our own lives and our futures, and to start creating for ourselves the changes which we wish to see. It is time to examine our lifestyles – the food we eat, our securities, our dependencies, our networks, our finances and so on –

and to be truly honest with ourselves. As I outline in Part Two, many people are already creating change through starting community projects and forming new networks. Within this – our Bridge Generation – the rising has already begun.

The future is going to be about the people on the ground. It will be about the changes each of us makes in our lives to be more aligned with moving forward. It will be about how resilient we are to the shocks/changes that are coming. It will be about how to cultivate a focused and positive state of mind and being. And importantly, it will be a question of how to be inherently spiritual in ourselves yet practical in our applications. Transitional periods are not normal times – they are periods when individual action can have much greater impact on historical developments. Yet true monastics not only operate as efficient workers on their own – they also know how to come together. There is a tale that illustrates this, which I call the *Meeting of Tools*:

> It is told that there was once a carpentry shed where all the tools held a meeting to settle their differences. At the head of this strange assembly was the hammer acting as president, but soon the other tools declared that he had to resign because he made too much noise with his blows. Hammer admitted the charge but he refused to resign from the presidency because it would mess up the organization, and if the screwdriver took over, as he was wanting to do, this would only screw things up and make the meeting chaotic and

without order. The screwdriver and all kinds of nails argued against this, while at the same time objecting to the sandpaper taking the presidency as this would create excessive friction with his usual rough treatment. Others agreed with this, and also said that the tape measure should be thrown out of the meeting as he always evaluated others according to a fixed pattern, as if he were the only one who was perfect.

Finally, the carpenter arrived, put on his apron and set about his work. He used the hammer, sandpaper, tape measure, nails and screws. Finally, the initial block of rough wood turned into a beautiful and useful piece of furniture. When the work was finished the carpenter silently left the room, and once again the tools' meeting was resumed. That was when the saw began to speak. He said:

'Friends, it has been shown to us that we each have our flaws, but the carpenter works with our qualities – that's what makes us valuable. Let us not think more on the negatives we see in each other; rather let us see the skills that we each contribute, and which the carpenter appreciates and uses to the best.'

The assembly then realized that the hammer was strong and gave force to the nails; sandpaper was able to polish and smooth things over; and the tape measure was accurate and precise. Together, they were a team capable of producing high-quality furniture. This made them proud of their strengths and capable of working together.

And from then on everyone became the best they could and worked in harmony to create the most beautiful and functional furniture one could ever hope to find.

As a global community of individuals we are being urged toward supporting a creative and shared developmental consciousness. Through a combination of physical changes on the social, cultural and political levels people all over the world are beginning to awaken to the recklessness inherent in our situation. From this there may be further 'awakenings' as the ironic, incredible and often absurd factors of many of our lifestyles are brazenly shown in the shocking light of current times.

In these upcoming years new monastics will continue to emerge throughout the world, becoming agents of change within communities. They will spread their influence through social networks – both physical and virtual. In order to 'change the world' we must first become change agents within ourselves. We must aspire toward a heightening of conscious awareness and intuitive understanding. Humanity is naturally integrative, and does not consciously seek to separate. Integral consciousness[2] is an aspect of the new monastics who are conscious of the underlying interconnectedness. Each person can be a part of this groundswell, with strong and confident voice and deeds, and yet devoid of ego and grand announcements. Such change catalysts can create meaning and significance in everything they do – even the small seemingly mundane things. Our modern modes of connectivity and communication can bring the new monastics into a networked gathering of heart–mind–spirit practical and visionary workers.

How difficult or easy the transition times will be depends much upon the response of each person. The keys to our collective development may very well have been planted within each of us, in our social sense of responsibility – in our innate urge to come together. The human species is, after all, a social species (as anthropologists keenly like to remind us!). It is easy to behave 'spiritually' when one is confined to the hermit's cave – then our only struggles are with our own ceaseless thoughts. Social participation is a responsibility to friends, family, community and to the wider world. It may well be that as times become more testing for many people the emphasis will shift toward the need for more integrated communities. Whatever the circumstances, much will be expected from people in the coming years as they face increased challenges and uncertainties – situations for which history holds few guidelines and precedents. The new monastics will be needed more than ever.

We must now accept that there is great need to 'Work' – to recalibrate and reinvigorate our relationship with the world we live in. This is not a time to fear for loss, but rather a time to aspire to new possibilities; to bring in new air, new potentialities and new gains. There is no clinging to the old when there is much vigorous work to be done. In this way, the new monastics will help to seed the coming generations that will be born *as* change – the Phoenix Generation – whilst being a pivotal part of the transitional Bridge Generation.

Chapter 4

The Bridge Generation

'If you seek small things to do, and do them well, great things will seek you, and demand to be performed.'
  Ancient saying

The pivotal years of the transition are crucial in order to 'hold the fort' and create stability and a degree of coherence as the old system energies die hard. And they will not die away overnight. Some of the current misunderstandings over the transition or 'energy shift' have been related to specific dates and so-called ancient calendars. Whilst a profound socio-cultural transition has emerged, it is not like a light switch that at one moment is suddenly and dramatically turned on and the whole place becomes illuminated. What we are dealing with here is not an instant struck-by-lightning effect. It is generational change that is happening swiftly when seen within the context of evolutionary time. Each generation will take part in the change, thus building an energy impulse. As mentioned before, we are not dealing here with linear change – these are the old patterns. As change builds upon change, each step will create exponential development. The current generations will feel and experience the shudders and shakes as we prepare the ground for those to come. This means being the bridge for later generations to arrive: specifically, for those who will be born *as* change. This means developing the capacity to view both the old and the new realities, and allowing the latter to emerge without the former collapsing into chaos.

Many of us are likely to experience living through a time of decreasing physical resources and finances. There are also likely to be emotional and psychological impacts that could be destabilizing. Some of the younger people within the Bridge Generation are already experiencing a hard time, as social and educational impacts serve to destabilize and confuse rather than support their personal development. Mainstream media outlets too bear a lot of responsibility for promoting unhealthy and disharmonious influences. According to researchers, children under the age of four who watch television are 20% more likely to develop attention-deficit disorder (ADD) by the age of seven than children who don't.[1] Some of the most widespread modern disorders affecting young people today are markedly anti-social traits: ADD, ADHD (attention-deficit hyperactivity disorder), ODD (oppositional-defiance disorder), PDD (pervasive developmental disorder), AS (Asperger syndrome), SID (sensory-integration dysfunction), and ASD (autistic spectrum disorder). In the USA one out of ten young people show signs of mental illness and more than 7 million have been diagnosed with ADD; diagnoses of ADHD are up 600% since 1990 and autism is now considered an epidemic.[2] Our young children are the fastest-growing segment of the prescription drug market, coerced into the need to consume Ritalin, Prozac or Risperdal. The controversial drug Ritalin has been reported to affect a child's size and weight, and to cause permanent changes to the brain. Prozac has been known to cause violent behaviour and is said to carry a high incidence of depression and suicide. Our young generations, who are the most vulnerable to narcotic influences, are being targeted by powerful medications that are supposed to represent the legal side of our societies. We can also add to this mix the barrage of soft drinks (with aspartame sweetner), junk food, alcohol, toxic pollutants, food additives and chemically treated material that increasingly pervade the environments that young children are exposed to as they grow up. It is not without coincidence that in recent years there also has been a marked increase in the number of children suffering from food allergies and nutrition disorders. Conditions include, but are not limited to, thyroid disorders, amino-acid deficiencies, inflamed intestines, and immune-system disturbances from the ingestion of pesticides, growth hormones, irradiated food and so on.

Also worrying is that our young generations are becoming ever more desensitized to extreme violence as video games increasingly merge with military simulations. Children's entertainment has gradually changed into 'militainment' as warfare gaming and first-person shooters become bestsellers and a gaming phenomenon. The simulation of violence and military machismo makes macabre, unreal and deviant fantasies realizable. Immersion is permitted at the press of a button; and instant on-demand gratifications satiate anti-social urges. It can become all too easy for an impressionable youngster to blur the boundaries between violent fantasy and the physical world. We must look at the shocking occasions when youngsters have violently taken the lives of others at school shootings. High-profile incidents in recent years include Sandy Hook Elementary School (2012); Virginia Polytechnic and State University (2007); and Columbine High School (1999), to name a few. Living through the current years may present difficulties as some of us struggle to embrace positive development amidst signs of imbalance. Yet this chaotic mixture is part of the process of change, and one that must be embraced and transformed from within. Those of the Bridge Generation have the responsibility, and privilege, of working from within the old system – using its models and energies in order to transform them. Thus, each individual has the task to live for those beyond their ego-self. As the philosopher Sri Aurobindo noted, the law for the individual is 'to harmonize his life with the life of the social aggregate and to pour himself out as a force for growth and perfection on humanity'.[3]

The impacts we can expect to receive in the coming years should also encourage us to increase our intent and focus in order to achieve and get things done on less – more through less. We may be forced – as well as encouraged – to live with less reliance on monetary trans-actions, and to seek alternative tangible lifestyles and status signifiers. It is generally in such times of transition that the notion of self-realization comes more consciously to the surface, alongside the psychological tendency toward collective, communal consciousness. With modern technologies bringing people into closer communication, there is also the tendency to find ourselves in relations that require greater awareness and tolerance. At the same time this process is forcing each one of us not only to know ourselves better, but also to know more profoundly those others to whom we are connected. Within the Bridge Generation we are experiencing the diffusion of knowledge and information with an unprecedented rapidity and scale. Human capacity is being catalyzed to respond to these changes and challenges.

Those of us who accept to walk upon and maintain this bridge will be asked to speak the language of transition clearly and calmly, both the language/vocabulary of the old systems and patterns and the new. The path will connect to both sides during the transition. For this reason, working on it requires sincerity, integrity and transparency. It is less about reliance upon external devices, and more about trusting one's inner self and instincts. That is why I feel that the Bridge Generation is on a warrior's path, in that it must be both strong and sincere, and yet subtle. It is a path that aligns both male and female energies, consciousness and values. The new values of connection, communication, consciousness and compassion, will assist us in aligning with an energy that binds rather than breaks, that emphasizes well-being as well as well-doing.

In this respect the value of sincerity is of great importance, now more than ever, as we are surrounded by tales, stories and false mythologies selling us pseudo-spiritual escapism or commercialized fear. The reality (or the 'greater truth') of this is more subtle and yet more powerful – it is the ongoing development of human society and the evolution of human consciousness. And it *is* an ongoing work in progress – and it is as simple and as difficult as that.

The Living Work

Welcome to the 21st century where communications and human stories are connecting us together like never before. The Internet represents aspects of this new relational 'feminine' energy. The Internet connects people into multiple relationships; it is responsible for nurturing rising empathy across the world; it shares stories and needs, and reaches out to many people and communities. Sure, it has its negative aspects too – that is the nature of a world of duality. If we focus on the constructive changes we see how individuals, communities, businesses and systems are recalibrating across the world to be aligned with the new interconnectivity that symbolizes the world we are moving into. This feminine energy needs new pathways in order to enter and permeate our material world. Our physical systems are responding to this call by shifting from centralized infrastructures to distributed and decentralized networks. Yet we also need to assist this recalibration by changing the ways we think since altering the ways we do things will not gain permanence until human consciousness changes. In order to allow the new changes to establish we need to allow the energies of change to flow through us. That is, to manifest the qualities, attitudes and our presence in the world that will most effectively receive, hold and transmit this perception and awareness. This responsibility is our living work now.

Remember our history lessons of the witchhunts and witch trials – remember stories of Salem? In the 16th– 18th centuries Europe witnessed a peak in the witchhunts that put to death tens of thousands of women accused of being witches. The executioners were predominantly men who represented the church hierarchy. This was a masculine energy that for millennia had been parading and swinging its heavy paternal axe of hierarchical power. The witches were a manifestation of female power that the ecclesiastical authorities could not tolerate. Many of these so-called 'witches' were women who knew about herbs, how to heal and nurture people, and how to listen to nature (others of course were victims of gossip). Yet one of the things they were accused of, amongst many, was of gathering and conspiring together. How did they gather? They gathered in witches' *circles* – here we have the energy of hierarchical power against the energy of circular, relational flow. It was the fear of a 'magical presence' within the female that fuelled a deep repression over the centuries that has become a pattern – the denial of the subtle, the integral, the nurturing. Now it is coming around again.

The new energy of this 'living work' is relational,

not mechanical nor isolated; it does not thrive upon seclusion but upon contact and receptivity through others. It flows and works through organic, non-hierarchical systems, through networks, webs, and circles, through the threads that weave the wholeness of life together. This energy does not thrive through top-down power structures; it no longer seeks one-to-one encounters – it flows like life itself. The days of working in seclusion are over – the new energy does not support separation. The flow must connect between inner and outer events and states. The new living work must exist within the active folds, avenues and marketplace of life. High castles, priestly enclaves, guru sanctuaries and all such are edifices of the past where a different energy was contained. The new energy – which shows aspects of the feminine consciousness – is a nurturing one that comes alive *through people.* Whereas the previous masculine-orientated energy wished to stand visible and powerful like the tower on the hill, the feminine energy is more subtle, and flows through the appreciative touch, the supportive word, the reassuring glance that filters through each one of us as we wend our way through life. That which was once hidden can now be made manifest through us – this is the *living work.*

So we need to be sincere with ourselves, for if *we* are unable to be, then who can do it for us? This sincerity means acknowledging that no matter how the world *appears* to be – external to us – the real work begins *within* us. And the real work does not arrive with a megaphone announcement, with fee-paying 'instant enlightenment' courses, or with emotionally stimulating/ gratifying commercial events. Often, such subtle work begins with a silence, a quietness of acknowledgement, attention, concentration, inspiration and intention. The process of transition and transformation requires patience from us for it is generational change, and we are in the midst of this process right now.

Conscious awareness is a new tool for us. We are only now really learning how to deal with its presence. This does not mean that the growth of conscious awareness is going to turn us into a psychic species overnight (remember what I said about our 'switching on the light' mentality?!). Yet it does mean that we will be feeling greater impulses and sparks of intuition – and we should trust more in those internal senses. They will turn out to be right more times than not – if we are listening correctly. This means being able to recognize what is appropriate for the time, and dismissing that which we feel is either no longer appropriate for us, or no longer relevant, or not in correct alignment with our new values. It is about accepting the responsibility to stand up for a new energy we are carrying around with us. I don't wish this to sound obscure or, heaven forbid, esoteric(!), yet we need to become accustomed to talking about the *feel* of the energies we carry around within us. When we are aware and attentive to our energy states we will instinctively feel when something is right or not. The growing sense within each person about what is right, appropriate and functional will start to shift potentials away from the power of institutions and more toward individuals. This is why it is important that individuals connect through emerging models of collaboration, such as social networks and new communication technologies.

Transition signifies a re-organization: a shifting of energies as well as physical systems, worldviews, perceptions and lifestyles. And in the midst of such 'spring cleaning', we need to be prepared to be adaptive, flexible and open for positive developmental change. Why should this be so difficult a concept to grasp? After all, we wouldn't spring-clean the house without first taking out or re-arranging the furniture. So why should it be so different for us? We need to re-arrange the furniture of our thinking, beliefs and models in order to welcome in the new arrangements. After this, we can learn to appreciate that things can – and will – get better. First, we just have to deal with the potential discomfort – and the responsibility – of grand planetary change. We need to respond to the 'calling'.

The Calling

There is one thing in this world you must never forget to do. If you forget everything else and do this one thing, you will have accomplished everything. Yet if you remember everything else and forget this one thing, then you will have done nothing in your life. *Rumi*

The 13th-century Persian poet Jalal ad-Din Rumi reminds us in the above saying that we have each arrived here in our lives with something to accomplish. This is our 'calling' – the inner impulse which urges us onward, often toward an unknown, or unrealized, destination.

Many people in the Bridge Generation will feel the stirrings of a 'calling': a need to activate something – some purpose or meaning – within them. Some may be attracted to books (such as this one), or to events, gatherings or other signifiers. Other ways to activate a person's calling – or *actualized* state – may come through *doing*; whilst others will be through *being*. Part of the process of opening ourselves up to what I have named abstractly as the 'calling' will be the need to prepare our minds to be receptive to new avenues of possibilities and potentials.

The Bridge Generation does not yet possess a common story, or even a shared consciousness. Yet these aspects within humanity are slowly beginning to emerge in mass – and not just in isolated, individual pockets as in times past. As we awaken we can begin to connect through our social technologies, and begin to build new potentials from our inherent connectivity. The awakener – as the lone inventor – can now connect with other like-minded (like-hearted and like-spirited) persons across the planet and begin seeding the energies of creative intention and change. We no longer have to work alone – by sharing what we know and feel, and what inspires us, we can participate in developmental change.

Change upon this planet will come through us, the people – and the attitudes, awareness, compassion, sincerity and related qualities that we embody and manifest. This is the real stability that can be passed on to those around us. As balanced, subtle, uplifting energies manifest in more and more people, change will increasingly occur in our external environments. Again, it will not appear overnight. Yet the energies are moving in the right direction, and there are millions of people already feeling this joy of change. The Bridge Generation needs to maintain a focus on the great opportunities emerging now and not become disheartened: as the infamous phrase puts it: *Illegitimi non carborundum* ('Don't let the bastards grind you down'). People's minds are changing all over the world, and with this come remarkable and inspiring potential and opportunity. Things can no longer go on as they have been; this is now plainly obvious to most observant people.

If you are reading these words now, it is because you are ready for this change and responsibility – and have the capacity to participate. Generational change is just that – it takes place over generations. Sounds like a long time? Well, in evolutionary terms we are zipping along. We are witnessing exponential change that would have awed our ancestors and should make our descendants proud. The Bridge Generation is already busy preparing and planting the seeds for a better Earth – no time to stop now. As Llewellyn Vaughan-Lee says, 'Love has no power structures or hierarchies; it is not for sale. It passes freely from heart to heart along the web of oneness that connects us all.'[4]

An important step in developing the potential and capacities within us is to become more conscious and aware of the abilities we already possess, and of their

61

presence within our daily lives. By learning how to manifest our intuition and inner feelings with conscious intent we will further facilitate their growth and functioning. Many people within the Bridge Generation may believe that tangible change is not occurring fast enough – especially when their instinct feels the need for changing the status quo. Yet we must acknowledge and accept the necessary learning process, and not be discouraged. We have sought power for ourselves from without – from our sciences and technology – to the detriment of our own inherent power that resides within. However, the reality that change is now moving through human society is evidenced by the dramatic increase in the number of people interested and committed to self-actualization, and the rise in human-potential movements. The urge is now rising strongly within many people. These stirrings will form the bedrock of the Bridge Generation, and allow us to prepare for future years that will not be based upon the past patterns. This new era of psycho-spiritual growth will be increasingly validated as new narratives and stories replace the old to ascribe to us a more truthful role in the evolutionary drama.

This new narrative is one of an evolving species within an evolving universe – a great adventure that is irreversible yet creative and inspiring. The Bridge Generation will see the signs of a new form of spirituality emerging, in which old institutional dogmas are replaced by increasing individual spiritual knowledge. The manifestation of spiritual truths will shift more into the open as inner intuition becomes stronger within each of us. We are moving toward the empowerment of the individual – of each human being – and this is frightening for the controlling authority structures. There will come a time, and it is already happening now, when the corruption within our social systems will become so blatant to all that no one can publicly deny it without ridicule or outrage. This is the new-consciousness shift toward transparency – and this will increase and manifest more strongly within the hearts and minds of the younger generations. The necessary shift toward increasingly transparent relations in our politics, society and economy will require the growing self-realization of the people. As people begin to become more actively aware and engaged in creating well-being, peace and social betterment, the changes will roll out exponentially. Those people already playing the part of the Bridge Generation are creating this platform for new models, innovations and ideas to spread.

In the next section I discuss how humanity is hard-wired to adapt biologically in response to experience, and how new neural processes in our brains can come into being through our changing forms of interactions, connections and communications. We are witness to a new global mind rising that is empathic, increasingly aware and eager to recalibrate.

The future is exciting – and it is right here where you are sitting . . .

part two

NEW MIND RISING

Part Two examines how humanity is benefiting from and developing its extended connectivity and communication networks. It explains how humanity is hard-wired to adapt physically in response to emerging global networks of connection and collaboration. The three chapters in this section discuss how people interact with new technologies; the impacts of social media; new emerging youth groups; and the rise of a global empathic mind. The influences of new social patterns of connectivity are giving rise to an increased planetary empathic awareness. The power of energetically connected individuals is fuelling the 'We' feeling and bringing the disenchanted together to develop their networks. We are witnessing the increasing rise of the maverick tinkerers, innovators and creative minds. These advancing new models are pushing against the old self-centred, vertical control systems. The new systems are showing that a different type of mind is arising, which will mark the generations to come.

Chapter 5

The Global Empathic Mind

The individual has to live in humanity as well as humanity in the individual.

Sri Aurobindo

The accelerating changes referred to in Part One will have no alternative but to force a mind-change on a global and individual level. We are coming together as a global species like never before, despite what we have been shown and told by the mainstream media. We need to view this in both the immediate and the bigger picture. Due to our relatively short human lifespan we rarely reflect beyond a generation or two behind us and in front of us. We have evolved as a species that reacts to immediate concerns; we have an ingrained myopic vision. This served us well in the past when we had survival needs in a restricted world of limited horizons. Yet now we need a perspective that is global at the very least – and even possibly beyond! We are accustomed to perceiving that which we see, touch, hear and feel; yet biologically we are also hard-wired to perceive through senses we may not ordinarily be aware of. In recent years neuroscience has discovered that humans also share sensory impacts with others (human and non-human) through what have been termed 'mirror neurons'.

A 'mirror neuron' is a brain neuron that is activated ('fires') when a living being (such as humans, primates and other mammals) observes the action of another. In other words, if an individual watches another person eat an apple, then the same brain neurons will fire in the person observing the action as if they themselves were performing the act. In humans such neuron behaviour has been found to operate in the premotor cortex and inferior parietal cortex. In a series of experiments a group of people were hooked up for brain scans (fMRI) and watched other people. The subjects' somatosensory cortex was activated by observing the others being touched. This discovery has led many notable neuroscientists to declare that mirror neurons are important for learning processes (imitation) as well as language acquisition. We might also say that this capacity is what ties a person in sympathy and empathy to another's situation. It could explain why people become so emotionally attached to events on television, and even cry in response to watching someone crying on the screen. In this way we are emotionally entangled through a mirroring of neuronal firing in the brain. If we expand this under-standing to take in worldwide events through global communications and social networks we can say that people are increasing their 'empathic entanglement'. Perhaps this goes some way to explaining the features of what has been recently termed the 'Global Brain' – a connected planetary nervous system.

If we now look at the bigger picture we will see that a different type of consciousness has been in emergence over the past 150 years, since the dawn of the Second Industrial Revolution. The new technologies of the Second Industrial Revolution – the telephone, radar, cinema, automobile and aircraft – called for a re-orientation of human perspective. A new perception of the dimensions of space and time began to give birth to a psychological consciousness – one that wanted to look beyond the borders and horizons of the physical frontier. The end of the 19th century was also a significant period in the rise of spiritualism and mediums, esoteric studies and the public emergence of occult movements.

As a brief overview, the 1870s onwards saw a peak in the growth of spiritualism in English-speaking countries. Interest was rife in communicating with the dead, contacting the afterlife, and believing in information from the astral plane. At the same time that interest in spiritualism was peaking, the Theosophical Society was established in New York City by Helena Blavatsky, Henry Olcott and William Judge in 1875. Theosophy heralded a revival in Western occultism and in the search for perennial wisdom. It was also a forerunner to later movements that sought to bring Eastern teachings and traditions to a Western audience. Theosophy has had a large impact upon Western mysticism as it brought forth many people who later founded their own individual channels for teaching, most notably Annie Besant, Alice Bailey, Krishnamurti and Rudolf Steiner.

The same period of the late 19th and early 20th centuries also saw the founding of the Hermetic Order of the Golden Dawn, and the emergence of esoteric figures such as Aleister Crowley, and G I Gurdjieff. In 1920 Paramahansa Yogananda arrived in the USA and established the Self-Realization Fellowship, and would go on to introduce thousands of Westerners to the art of meditation and yoga. In 1946 Yogananda published the phenomenally successful *Autobiography of a Yogi* which has sold millions of copies worldwide. Other personages gathering devotees and spreading teachings throughout the West at this time include Sri Aurobindo, Hazrat Inayat Khan and Sri Meher Baba, amongst others. Soon a whole range of Asian mystical and occult teachings became better known within Western society, as well as creating bridges to Eastern ashrams and religious centres.

It was not by accident that at this time there also emerged a great wave of influence that turned people's thinking towards a more interiorized, as well as a more transcendental, state. This encouraged a shift from the physical realm towards a belief in, and an exposure to, non-physical realms. The shift towards a more intuitive reasoning was also marked by the rise of the American Transcendentalism movement in New England in the first half of the 19th century, with notable figures such as Ralph Waldo Emerson, Henry David Thoreau, Walt Whitman and Margaret Fuller. This movement reacted against religious dogma and over-intellectualism and sought to find truths through direct inner experience. The transcendentalists aimed to trust an internal 'knowing' and subjective experience of events rather than working through external impacts alone.

These explorations were further advanced by the Canadian psychiatrist Richard Bucke (*Cosmic Consciousness: A Study in the Evolution of the Human Mind*, 1901); and Harvard psychologist William James (*The Varieties of Religious Experience: A Study in Human Nature*, 1902). These ideas were beginning to circulate amongst an educated public at the same time that psychoanalysis, developed in Vienna in the 1890s by Sigmund Freud, was also percolating into mainstream circles. The early part of the 20th century was a period when the 'collective unconscious' was becoming a recognized part of the collective mind. The theories of Freud, Jung, Reich and other psychoanalysts were changing how people regarded human behaviour and revising the parameters of human thinking. Early childhood impacts, experiences, repressions and sexuality were all now being unearthed as contributing to the contours of the human mind. What happened 'out there' was recognized as being a manifestation of what was going on inside a person's inner realm.

These developments coincided with the rise of the motion pictures – a way of projecting ideas onto an external screen – as a cultural phenomenon. Philosophy too was taking on new ideas that included a creative 'vitalism' within the human, Nature's holism, and the patterns of flow within the universe.[1] Yet perhaps the most revolutionary change in 20th-century human thinking came about in the realm of physics, specifically the emergence of quantum mechanics. Quantum physics presented to the world the concepts of particle-wave duality, nonlocality, observer interference and wave collapse. Suddenly, the world was not as fixed, durable or mechanical as previously thought. It was now seen as an unpredictable, uncertain, energetic sea of chance: God did, it seems, play dice after all.

The 20th century thus became a time for asking and answering such questions as: What lies beyond life? What is behind matter? What lies behind our conscious thoughts? What lies behind all biological life? This quest for human meaning in both outer and inner realms permeated the zeitgeist in the second half of the 20th century as the East came to meet the West.

A Western counterculture was now emerging through the new-found popularity of Eastern teachings (Buddhism, Taoism, Sufism and others) and the play-fulness of mind-altering processes. Significantly, during this period of experimental cultural expression, a new form of psychological consciousness was being explored. Through psychoanalysis and the theories of Freud, the 1950s and 1960s opened up new areas of self-evaluation. People were increasingly investigating their own feelings through self-reflection and the interior gaze. Timothy Leary was right to suggest that the new era had shifted to 'the politics of the nervous system'. This search for non-ordinary states of consciousness also led to many Westerners seeking out a shamanic training. The market place was open for experimenting with human potential. Interest in transpersonal issues, interior realms and metaphysics opened the door to a dramatic surge in forms of spiritual belief quickly labelled as 'New Age'. These included studies of life after death, past lives, angels, auras, channelling, divination, crystals, the *I-Ching*, spiritual healing, prayer circles, holism, spirit guides, and more. There was also a surge of interest in the ancient esoteric interests of alchemy, Hermeticism, the Kabbalah and Gnosticism.

The power of change brought about the eventual collapse of the Soviet Union and the fall of the Berlin Wall in 1989/90. By the 1990s the best-selling poet in the United States was the Persian Sufi Rumi; holography and the holographic universe was a common new interest; the left–right working of the brain hemispheres was a popular subject; the Internet was revolutionizing communications; and notions such as the noosphere, Global Brain, and collective consciousness were almost commonplace. What a revolution of human thought in such a short span of social history!

These changes all correlated with a greater shift toward individual responsibility; a deepened sense of self and psychological reflection; an increased sensitivity to internal and external states; and a heightened recognition and appreciation of human community. They set the stage for long-term growth in the psychological evolution of the human self. These developments also sowed fertile soil for those of the Bridge Generation who will form a core of transformation over the coming years.

The period of psycho-spiritual transformation that will unfold over the coming years will deliver impulses for radical social change and cultural renovation, alongside innovation in science, energy and social technologies. Our human perceptions too are awakening to an understanding that our place within the larger cosmos is anything but inanimate, unconscious and accidental. We are set to witness a generation waking up, with new arrivals being born *into* change and heralding the later wave of those who will be born *as* change. Within these years an increased drive for human betterment will manifest that will be marked through intensified activism for social, political and ecological change, and for changes in the balance of global power. The active presence of many international socio-cultural-political movements will also release much concentrated energy for creative transition.

The spectacular rise in global communication technologies reflects a new form of participatory consciousness, especially among younger people. This new model is a distributed one; in other words, it connects people through networks rather than through hierarchical structures. It also represents a more feminine energy that seeks relationships, to nurture and to collaborate rather than compete and conquer. This emerging feminine energy underlies the rise in global empathy. Also, since people are connecting amongst themselves in multiple relationships it impels them to have an active engagement. For those individuals brought up within the older generation of communication technologies (radio, television, fixed phones), the interaction was at most two-way, and for the most part one-way. In that era people were passive receivers, targeted with a limited spectrum of information they could not engage with. This has now shifted so that the receiver of the communication is both the *user* and the *producer*. We have learnt to democratize our engagement and to activate choice through online social networks, phone messaging, video channels and various other broadcast mediums. The generation waking up is learning fast how to set up inexpensive, or free, radio sites (podcasts), home websites or newsletters, and they are now orchestrating and managing their own forms of voice and self-expression.

This new model of communication and connection can be said to be rewiring our thinking and behaviour patterns. We are becoming accustomed to dealing with multiple connections rather than single ones, and to becoming immersed in varied and diverse relations and not just one-on-one dialogues. In turn we are being exposed to, and impacted by, a myriad of viewpoints, beliefs, identities and experiences. Within these models of self-expression each person is being called forth to respond and engage with the outside world not in fear or with anxiety but with healthy, creative and positive energies. This exposure to new patterns of information is helping to re-pattern both our social lives as well as our brain neurons.

Many of us are forming new priorities in our lives as we restructure our social networks to incorporate new modes of interpersonal relations. Social connectivity has developed and matured tremendously over the past decade. As well as online networks, forums and meeting places, there are thousands of international non-profit and non-governmental organizations. A form of collective social intelligence is beginning to manifest, but it is not from the centre.

The creative impetus for change will not emerge from any centre, as did the Renaissance that sprang up in northern Italy in the Late Middle Ages. The new 'renaissance' is likely to manifest not from one specific geographical location but from distributed networks around the world as conscious individuals and groups connect, network and collaborate. These conscious and creative groups will spread their influence through decentralized connections like ink dots on blotting paper until a time comes when the dots begin to fill the paper and change its colour. Many social changes in the coming years will emerge from the creative engagement and innovation of individuals and collectives worldwide – a shift catalyzed within the hearts, spirit and minds of the people.

Externally we may seem like a vast, distant and separate collection of individuals; yet in truth the human family is an intimate, closely entwined species comprised of various cultures. Many of the younger generation are now waking up to this fact. Youngsters the world over are growing up accustomed to having networks of hundreds, perhaps even thousands, of friends across the planet, sharing intimacy and empathizing easily with an international social group of like-minded souls. This younger generation is manifesting, whether conscious of it or not, a nonlocal level of human relationships.

This expanded connectivity is bringing about a change in our psychology and consciousness. We are now being impelled to live in ways that enable all other people to live equally well. We are also being compelled to live in ways that respect the lives of others; that respect the right of all people to economic and cultural development; and that pursue personal fulfilment in harmony with the integrity of nature. These traits constitute what I refer to as an integral–ecological consciousness, shown in people acting and behaving as both individuals and as parts of the greater connected whole. Such multiple relations form a more varied, rich and complex life; they provide a more diverse range of activities than before and encourage relationships that stretch the self. As well as providing challenges for developing new skills and learning, our diverse networks can help us form new friendships and add extra meaning to our lives.

As a new global empathic mind emerges, people worldwide will grow up with new expressions of mindfulness that are more caring, relational and feminine in energy. The 21st century is likely to be an era that births and nurtures such an evolving consciousness. The 20th century's exploration of the psyche – as briefly outlined above – is mixing with today's communication networks to herald a more reflexive mode of self-expression. People today are comfortable in expressing themselves with strangers; they explore and express their inner thoughts, feelings, emotions and ideas with hundreds of unknown persons online, from various cultural backgrounds. More and more daily interactions are empathic as we react and share news, stories and emotional impacts from sources around the world.

Empathy is one of the core values by which we create and sustain social life. Exposure to impacts outside our own local and restrictive environments helps us to learn tolerance, and to live with experiences that are richer and more complex, full of ambiguities and multiple perspectives. It is a mode of connecting that allows diverse people worldwide to construct a new form of planetary social capital. Just as in our smaller, often ancient communities, where cultural/social capital preceded commercial capital, we have the resources to co-create a planetary human society where once again the focus is on social benefit rather than profit. We can see the emerging models of this in modern variations today, such as in open-source software like Linux, or in collaborative tools such as Wikipedia. The online global commons is a model for the new paradigm that illustrates how sharing can work above the individual thrust for profit and commercial gain. The values and ethics of communal sharing might seem odd or out of place to the old capitalist–consumerist mindset, yet these are the very values that will be on the rise in the coming generations.

During this phase of our socio-cultural and self development we are being challenged to expand and evolve our mental, emotional and perceptual faculties. The psychological interactions available today for the young people growing up with a global/planetary aware-ness are without precedent. More and more young people are growing up experiencing social relationships that transcend space and time, as well as cultures, national boundaries and local ideologies. This may account for the increasing numbers of young people in developed nations becoming involved in community and social projects and NGOs, such as by taking a year out to help in another culture abroad, to learn, experience and to offer assistance. Volunteering among the young, despite what appears to be the contrary, is on the increase. Young people are even putting themselves into dangerous situations – in conflict zones – to stand up for values of peace, justice, equality and human rights. Across the world young minds are demanding fair and equal access for all peoples to engage in open communication and free speech. This very issue is already a point of contention, with many governments, both Western and non-Western, attempting to curtail, firewall and monitor many of our present communication channels. However, the great advantage of networked communications is that such barriers can be circumvented by creative minds. And it appears that many more creative minds will be joining the global conversation as our current generations increasingly 'wake up'.

In 2012 the population was around 7 billion and the proportion of registered Internet users was 33%, five times more than a decade before. By 2020 world population is set to be 7.8 billion and Internet usage worldwide is predicted to reach 66% – that's a little under 3 billion new people plugging in to the global conversation. In other words, nearly 3 billion new minds will be tapping in to the information flows; and that's many millions of new creative problem solvers, innovators and visionaries. What is more, the majority of these new minds will be coming online from Asia, the Middle East and what have often been referred to as the developing countries. These will be mostly young minds, and minds with the urge for social betterment. Can we imagine the collective potential of these creative new minds, many of them thinking outside of the box, and outside of the old patterns?

The capacity for new minds to grasp, explore and develop from information was stunningly shown by the work of scientist and educationalist Sugata Mitra. Dr Mitra discovered that illiterate, uneducated and unsupervised children were able to teach themselves when provided with Internet access. As early as 1999 Mitra and his team carved a 'hole in the wall' that separated his research premises from the adjoining slum in Kalkaji, New Delhi. They installed a freely accessible computer in the hole for the slum dwellers to access on the other side, and the responses were videoed. It proved to be an instant hit especially among the young street children. With no prior experience, the children learnt to use the computer on their own. This prompted Mitra to believe that any group of children could learn through a process of 'incidental learning', as long as there was content, motivation and at times some minimal guidance.[2] In order to test his ideas further Mitra set up freely accessible computers in Shivpuri (a town in Madhya Pradesh) and in Madantusi (a village in Uttar Pradesh). These experiments came to be known as the 'Hole-in-the-Wall' experiments. The findings from Shivpuri and Madantusi confirmed the results of the Kalkaji trial. It appeared that the children in these two places picked up computer skills on their own. Dr Mitra has defined this as a new way of learning – Minimally Invasive Education. Mitra has subsequently established 'Learning Stations' throughout India and also outside India in other deprived areas. After many more years of vigorous research Mitra's results all show that children learn to operate as well as play with the computer with minimum intervention. They are also able to pick up new skills quickly and accomplish tasks by constructing their own learning environment. Imagine what many of these bright young minds will bring to the global conversation in the years to come?

As some measure of what to expect we can see now how young minds the world over are already participating in creating innovative change. For example, 12-year-old Steven Gonzalez Jr., who was diagnosed with acute myeloid leukaemia, a rare form of cancer, credits video games for helping him survive the experience. In wishing to help other cancer patients his age he then created a video game, *Play Against Cancer*, in which players destroy cancer cells illustrated as green ghosts. Gonzalez has also developed The Survivor Games, a social network and online community for teen cancer patients. Similarly, a group of four 14-year-old girls – who named themselves 'Team 2-the-Res-Q' developed CyberMentors, which is an anti-bullying Android app for young people that focuses on building self-esteem and increasing safety. The app also includes a messaging feature through which users can talk to a CyberMentor directly about experiences with bullying. Perhaps the youngest person to have been certified as developing a software gaming program is Zora Ball. At only seven years of age Zora not only created a mobile game app using the Bootstrap programming language, but was able to reconfigure her program on request to prove it was her own work. Although these are examples of technology-driven youngsters, it does show that there is a wave of young, creative minds waiting to arrive upon the planetary stage.[3] Furthermore, such young minds and hearts are demonstrating a strong desire to help and assist others, and are largely driven by altruistic urges. How technology is used in our hands will be crucial for the changes to come.

Consider also how a slum-dweller in Africa with a mobile phone now has potential access to better communications than did President Reagan 25 years ago. With a smart phone with Internet access and the use of search engines then the slum-dweller is likely to have better communications diversity than President Clinton 15 years ago. This is the power of exponential change. What is more, it is the young minds behind these technologies of communication that are the true power source. Imagine living in a world where a few humans can touch the lives of millions – it's already arrived! Our external connectivity is the exoskeleton mirroring the collective field of human consciousness (*see* next chapter). As more and more inspiring individuals add their ideas to the global conversation and envision the unexpected, this will undoubtedly inspire others to envision the previously thought impossible. These are signs of a strengthening empathic consciousness: a service-to-others as opposed to service-to-self. Such thinking and behaviour has the power to create great change as we are at a point in history when even small catalysts can produce monumental shifts.

It is significant that in times of relative social stability, human consciousness plays a lesser role in the behaviour of society. However, when societies reach the limits of their stability then they are sensitive and responsive to even the smallest fluctuations in the consciousness of their citizens. In such times, changes in values, belief sets, perceptions and so on hold great sway over the future direction of the social milieu. Human consciousness becomes a significant stimulus and catalyst for change during these times of social instability. That is why it is imperative that humanity be collectively focused upon development and betterment rather than coerced into a fear-based status quo. We should not underestimate the capacity for the human mind to adapt and evolve according to social and environmental impacts and influences. That is why our psycho-spiritual evolution is an unfinished project, and relies on people 'waking up' to stimulate new neuronal pathways.

How we communicate as social beings wires the neurons in our brains and in-forms our psyche. Thus, the shift to a networked exchange of information and human relationships has helped to usher in not only new forms of social organization but has also influenced how we have 'wired' our brains. When our mind and attention are focused in specific ways we create neural firing patterns that link and integrate with previously unconnected areas of the brain. In this way synaptic linkages are strengthened, the brain becomes more inter-connected, and the human mind becomes more adaptive.

Child development author Joseph Chilton Pearce has written about how several times during an infant/child's development the brain does a 'clean-up' by releasing a chemical that dissolves all unproductive, unused or redundant axon–dendrite connections. The result is that the productive and well-used neural fields are left intact.[4] In other words, if we don't use them we lose them! Further, he explains that a child of six years is provided by nature with a new spurt in brain growth, effectively boosting the neural connections by four to five times.

Yet such neural updates do not only occur during our childhood. According to psychologist Daniel Siegel the adult brain undergoes genetically programmed 'neural pruning sprees', which he says involve removing various neural connections to better organize brain circuitry. Again, this suggests that the neural connections that are no longer used become disconnected (deactivated), thus strengthening those regularly used synaptic connections, which helps the brain to operate more efficiently. As the phrase goes, neurons that fire together, wire together. By adapting to new social interactions and cross-cultural impacts we are sending signals to our brain to rewire itself according to new behavioural and thinking patterns.

Our modern sense of self-awareness has clearly evolved to root us in our social world, a world of extended relationships and social networks. Humanity, it can be said, has been biologically hard-wired to tap into extended social connections and communication networks. Our small tribal communities were only an earlier stage along this evolutionary path. We are also hard-wired to adapt physically in response to experience – new neural processes in our brains can come into being with intentional effort, awareness and different patterns of concentration. This capacity to create new neural connections, and thus new mental skill sets through experience, has been termed neuroplasticity. The human brain of today has to respond to the incredible amount of energy and information that is flowing through our environments and embedded in our cultural experiences. By being aware of our experiences and environmental impacts and influences we can gain a better understanding of how our brain and thinking becomes re-patterned. This awareness is what Siegel calls 'mindsight':

> In sum, experience creates the repeated neural firing that can lead to gene expression, protein production, and changes in both the genetic regulation of neurons and the structural connections in the brain. By harnessing the power of awareness to strategically stimulate the brain's firing, mindsight enables us to voluntarily change a firing pattern that was laid down involuntarily.[5]

Thus, how we focus our attention and awareness greatly shapes the structure of our brains. Further, the ability to grow new neural connections is available throughout our lives and not only in our young formative years. This knowledge encourages us to nurture our mindfulness, our self-awareness and our empathic relations with others. Neuroplasticity also encourages us to pay more attention to our human networks, and to develop those social skills that underlie empathy and compassion. These new 'wired connections' are exactly what are becoming activated as individuals increasingly 'wake up' to what is happening within our communities and societies and upon the planet. Such distributed connections breach cultural and national borders and force us to self-reflect on our identity, values and ethics. The exoskeleton of our global communications is in turn catalyzing new patterns and organization within the human psyche. These emerging energy patterns are likely to have traits of a feminine consciousness, using energies that work through relationships rather than one-on-one; that seek to nurture co-operation; and that are nourished themselves through compassion and loving connections.

As a species we are being prepared for connectivity within a shared global empathic mind in order to evolve parallel with an emerging new evolutionary era upon this planet.

New Minds Want Peace

A new narrative is emerging, one in which each person is integral to the larger picture; the journey of each one of us is a part of the journey as a whole. This new story informs us that the possibilities are open for humanity to engage in consciously creating its way forward – with harmony, balance and respect to all. This new narrative is part of humanity's evolving empathic mind and should compel us to seek greater connectivity and meaning in our lives. Many younger minds the world over are resonating and embracing a new consciousness of connection and compassion. The younger minds do not wish to be rote-fed the anger, fear and insecurity of their past generations. They want to reach out for change and betterment.

Around the world there are examples of young people rejecting the conflict mentality of their elder generations. In conflict zones especially, where young minds are conditioned into hatred of fixed enemies, there is a backlash against this old programming. Younger people are reaching out across artificial borders to engage with the so-called 'enemy' and to start a new dialogue of peace and reconciliation. Such minds realize that the conflict mentality has no future, and will be left behind if it cannot accept change. Whereas many of the old programmed minds thought that the future meant putting up borders, and viewing the 'others' with suspicious eyes, many of the young minds see differently. We can see this in youth movements worldwide as there is change emerging in the mindset of young people everywhere. This is especially so in Middle Eastern territories where restrictive regimes are now encountering rising youthful demographics who are not accepting the old mentalities and old ways. The young people want what almost everybody wants – peace, justice, equality, freedom. There is a new spring in the step of young, tech-savvy, energetic minds that are bypassing the old models (*see* Chapter 7). In the years ahead – at least for the next two decades – we will increasingly see the signs of the changing of the old guard. And this time they will not be replaced by those with the same consciousness. With generational change we will see the gradual transition to an era of individuals who think differently, feel differently, connect differently, and who will want to work toward a different world. This forms part of the psycho-spiritual evolution that will accompany the generational shift toward what I have called the Phoenix Generation.

One example of this generational change is the youth movement Generation Waking Up, which calls itself a 'global campaign to ignite a generation of young people to bring forth a thriving, just, sustainable world'. They announce that, 'A new generation of young people is waking up. We are the middle children of History, coming of age at the crossroads of civilization, a generation rising between an old world dying and a new world being born.'[6] Through their open-source, multi-media workshops, training and leadership academies Generation Waking Up (which refers to itself as 'GenUp') is mobilizing young people both locally and globally.[7] GenUp is part of a whole array of meetings, gatherings and workshops that are popping up all over the world and engaging young minds in new thinking and new futures. Such people are living as far into the future as they can in order to transform the present. As the visionary Buckminster Fuller once said:

> The youth of humanity all around our planet are intuitively revolting from all sovereignties and political ideologies. The youth of Earth are moving intuitively toward an utterly classless, raceless, omnicooperative, omniworld humanity.[8]

The opportunity for change and betterment exists like never before in our recent history. This means that there is also responsibility; and these two factors may never be present again at exactly the right moment when they are so badly needed. What the human species may now be witnessing is the rise of intuition, empathy, greater connectivity to the world and to people and a sense of 'knowing' what changes need to be made. Furthermore, within each person is a growing sense of the greater cosmic whole: the realization that humanity exists and evolves within a universe of great intelligence and meaning. This serves to impart to humanity a more profound spiritual impulse. We are on the evolutionary road to coming together as one.

Chapter 6

Coming Together as One

There can be no greater foolishness than to deny the reality of something only because one has not experienced it.
   Al Ghazzali

On 16–17 August 1987, the Harmonic Convergence gathering took place. This brought many people together to celebrate the planetary alignment that was then occurring. The aim of the gathering was to facilitate the shift towards a new era. Planet Earth was again placed as the central focus of people's thoughts. Perhaps not since the Apollo space programme, and the first photos of the Earth from space, had humanity been so focused on the blue dot. The iconic photo of Earth taken on 7 December 1972, by the crew of Apollo 17, has been instrumental in focusing peoples' minds toward unity consciousness. With the emergence – and *convergence* – of transcendental philosophies, ecological awareness, space travel and technologies that connect us over distance and time, the human psyche has been undergoing preparation for a new era of social organization and communication.

Recent decades especially have seen an advance in the ecological view of living systems and the interconnectedness and interaction between humans, nature and environment. Moreover, this shift toward integral thinking has also embraced the nonmaterial levels of the human psyche and consciousness. Through our various cultures, and with our recently created vocabulary of the psyche, we are developing the language, the skills and nuances to sense and articulate our personal, revelatory experiences. The inner 'shamanic' realm is being explored by more and more people within the contexts of their everyday lives. We are slowly learning to externalize our internal states. Even our new scientific discoveries are explaining and validating the energetic threads that connect our internal states with external reality. The latest in scientific discovery now confirms that there is no 'out there', and that all living beings are inherently enfolded within an energy entanglement. Up until now the dominant paradigm has been that the solid things we experience are real, and the space around them is empty and passive. However, science is now informing us that it is the space that is real, and the solid things that are secondary. This concept emerges from the findings of cutting-edge physics. Space, quantum physicists now realize, is not empty and passive but is a 'full' and dynamic field (even though some physicists still refer to it as the 'quantum vacuum'!).

Latest discoveries have found that atoms and particles (in the quantum state) can be instantly projected across any finite distance. This phenomenon is referred to as 'teleportation', and is already an intense research area for such things as secure quantum encryption in communications (with obvious military uses). It has also been found that instant quantum-resonance-based interactions operate in living systems, and in the known physical universe. What this means is that 'nonlocal' interaction (action at a distance) occurs between the parts or elements of systems and transcends the recognized bounds of space and time.

We have been conditioned to think of space as being the empty and passive background from which things manifest – or it is the 'nothingness' that hangs between objects. In fact, the truth is the reverse to this. It is the undulating cosmic matrix – which forms the background of what we refer to as space – that is real; and matter is a manifestation that emerges from this underlying reality. Perhaps a good way to visualize this is by the following analogy. When we look at the sea we think of waves as moving along the surface, toward the shore or spreading out behind ships. The waves appear to move from one point on the sea toward another. Yet in fact the molecules of water do not move laterally from one place to another – they only move up and down. The view of waves travelling across the surface of the sea is an optical effect. It is not the waves that travel across the sea, but rather the surface that fluctuates and gives the impression of rolling movement – like the shake of a blanket. This is the same for the quantum field of space – things do not move *across* or *over* space, they move within space. Everything is contained within the sea of immense underlying energy, from which matter emerges as a secondary phenomenon.

The vision the emerging paradigm gives us is very different from the still dominant vision. The world that meets our eye is not an illusion, but it is not what it appears to be either. The real world is not an arena of separate things moving across an empty space. All things manifested in our reality are conveyed in, and are a part of, a richly dense and dynamic energy matrix. This, however, does not mean that the existence of solid objects is an illusion, only that their separateness is. This may sound like science fiction to some people – yet it is quantum science fact. We can now state that reality, as we currently understand it, is a giant quantum system in which all things are intrinsically and instantly inter-connected. In a previous book I have referred to this paradigm as the 'Akashic Age'.[1]

On a biological level also, the latest research in the study of biophysics and biofields reveals that a form of quantum coherence is present within living biological systems. Biological coherence operates through what are known as biological excitations and biophoton emission. In this context 'coherence' refers to wave patterns that converge harmoniously. A popular example of this is the laser in which multiple waves of amplified light are directed in a narrow coherent beam of condensed and directed energy. Biophysics tells us that metabolic energy is stored as a form of electromechanical and electro-magnetic excitations. It is these coherent excitations that are considered responsible for generating and maintaining long-range order via the transformation of energy and very weak electromagnetic signals.[2]

Researcher Fritz-Albert Popp hypothesizes that bio-photons are emitted from a coherent electrodynamic field within the living system.[3] What this means is that each living cell is giving off, or resonating, a biophoton field of coherent energy. If each cell is emitting this field then this results in the whole living system becoming a resonating nonlocal energy field. This, claims Popp, is the basis for coherent biological organization – referred to as quantum coherence. Coherence, it appears, is the byword for living systems.

Relatively new developments in biophysics have also shown that DNA is a liquid crystal lattice-type structure (which some refer to as a liquid crystal gel) in which body cells are involved in a holographic instantaneous communication via the biophoton field. Moreover, biophysics has discovered that living organisms are permeated by quantum wave-forms. This incredible new information actually positions each living being within a nonlocal quantum field consisting of wave interferences (where bodies meet). The liquid crystalline structure within living systems is also responsible for the direct current (DC) electrodynamic field that permeates the bodies of all animals. It has also been noted that the DC field has a mode of semi-conduction that is much faster than the nervous system.[4]

Human consciousness, we now learn, is not only in a 'wave-interference' relationship with other mind-fields, but is also constantly transmitting and receiving information. Clinical psychiatrist Daniel Siegel notes how the body's neural networks operate as a form of 'extended mind' to receive and transmit data and sensory information. The body thus acts as a vital field source of intuition that powerfully influences our reasoning.[5]

Similarly, researchers at the Californian HeartMath Institute have been investigating cardiac coherence through exposure to specific emotions. It has been found that when a person experiences positive feelings like love, care, appreciation and joy, their electrocardiograph becomes coherent. On the other hand, when exposed to negative emotions like anger, worry or hostility, the electrocardiograph shows incoherent patterns. The phenomenon of biological coherence has been speculated to be the factor behind the transfer of healing energies between people. It has also been shown that people who meditate can achieve an extremely high level of cross-hemispheric synchronization. Similarly, people who mediate together have been discovered to synchronize their brain activity. Through the use of EEG brain scanning it has been shown that brainwave activity is synchronized amongst the participants in such groups. There have also been studies in which human neurons were separated and sealed in so-called Faraday containers in order to block out physical communication. Yet, when one set of neurons were stimulated with a laser, the other separated group of neurons registered the same changes at the same time. Former chief-of-staff of Medical City Dallas Hospital Larry Dossey refers to such phenomena as 'One Mind.'[6] Likewise, families may, according to some psychotherapists, possess a common shared emotional field; such as the established research proving brainwave correlations between the brains of identical twins. There are literally hundreds of verified scientific studies that show the inherent coherence between humans biologically, mentally, emotionally and energetically. The scientific validation of nonlocal fields of consciousness places greater emphasis upon our recognition of collective or group coherence within humanity.

As discussed in Chapter 5, the notion of mirror neurons and empathy are the forerunners to understanding our fundamental interconnectivity as a species. We are learning that extended fields of conscious information and communication exist between individuals and groups as a medium of coherence that may further entangle humanity into a collective 'grand family'. It is interesting to note how nowadays there are increasing numbers of people who are becoming sensitive to human fields of connectivity, whether through empathy-at-a-distance or, for example, perceiving the presence of subtle energy fields around others. Also, the general interest in metaphysical subjects these days has exploded, with a psychological language and mindset emerging to deal with these increasingly well-recognized phenomena. It is now becoming commonplace to speak of reiki, chi, pranic energy and even of quantum energy. Not only are many cultures and societies learning to deal with a modern wave of technological networks (as already discussed), but also with an increase in conscious awareness of human connections within an extended mind. In this way humanity is learning how to be a more interactive, empathic and collective extended family. Never before in the known history of our species have we come to a point where we are sailing in the same ship, afflicted by the same concerns, and affected similarly by a range of planet-wide impacts. The realization is now dawning on the peoples of the world: that we are all a part of the field fabric of a collective family.

This realization is being keenly felt, too, by the younger generations: generations that are growing up accustomed to sharing intimacy and empathizing easily with others internationally. This younger generation is manifesting, whether conscious of it or not, a non-local-field level of relationships. It is a form of energy resonance that mimics the quantum state of the particle and the wave: each person is clearly isolated from another by physical distance (particle), yet at the same time very much entangled in a conscious field of con-nectivity and communication (wave). In other words, each is participating in a field view of reality, a reality that creates an extended set of responsibilities as one's thoughts and actions can reverberate to greater distances. This then becomes a participative worldview, as inner experiential states connect with outer events and experiences. In this worldview the psychic aspect of reality becomes more dominant as the person integrates themselves into the fabric of the connected world rather than being an external participant. By immersing ourselves in the world as a whole we are embracing our empathic and compassionate communion.

We each have the choice – and *response*-ability – to develop consciously from each of our multiple interactions, whether face-to-face or at-a-distance. Sociologists have, up until now, been largely focused on human identity as characterized by individualization, especially so in 'modern/postmodern' societies in which the service-to-self attitude has been rampant. Yet this is a myopic vision on two counts: on one hand it neglects that humans instinctively seek groupings and attachments; and on the other it fails to recognize that the nature of human consciousness also undergoes change along with socio-cultural shifts. The hypothesis I put forward in this book is that, in accordance with our evolutionary trajectory, a new form of consciousness will emerge as new generations arrive on this planet. This new wave of consciousness will then gradually seep into the core of all our future societies.

These emerging states have already been appearing sporadically, often in exceptional individuals, although sometimes also as freak occurrences or after traumatic shocks. The transition at hand is for these infrequent manifestations of a new form of human consciousness to become more universal – toward a planetary integral consciousness. As I explain in Part Three, the Phoenix Generation will be perhaps the first wave of new arrivals to exhibit these patterns of consciousness – as a natural, organic progression. Eventually, the 'new age' will become the 'new normal' as new patterns of thinking and perception seep into the general collective consciousness. The new paradigm will wash over the old with its new models and new ways of doing things.

Already the integrated perspective is slowly percolating into our patterns of perception as more and more people embrace and instinctively trust non-material information. The dominant materialist worldview is under increased scrutiny as more people awaken to the possibility that their intuitive glimpses – dreams, visions, premonitions and so on – are reliable sources of information that originate from alternative senses. Through seeking practices that were once considered metaphysical, such as yoga, meditation, psychotherapy, transpersonal therapy, bio-feedback and altered states of consciousness, people are accessing a once hidden, or rather neglected, realm of senses and self-knowing. As more people realize that the subtle realm of extrasensory information is not a figment of fantasy or delusion, but in fact has a scientific foundation, these states of consciousness will become more widely accepted, and assimilated. Philosopher Ervin László notes that:

> In time, however, a more evolved consciousness is likely to spread over all the continents. It will spread by a form of contagion. An evolved mind is 'infectious', it affects less evolved minds . . . A more evolved consciousness will motivate people to develop their own consciousness, it will transform humanity's collective unconscious.[7]

Whilst the transition may not appear to unfold suddenly to us, within evolutionary terms it will be an exceptional surge. As we continue through these years of social and cultural change – of challenges to our worldview and models – we are almost certainly going to be coerced into rethinking and re-evaluating our perceptions and modes of conscious awareness.

Our latest scientific discoveries and technological innovations are helping to prepare humanity for the realization that meaningful relationships can operate at a distance. Dynamic and empathic connections can manifest through nonlocal fields of exchange. It is as if we are initially manifesting outwardly – *exteriorizing* – our inherent internal attributes as a pre-model, or type of blueprint. We are establishing the exoskeleton of human entanglement around the planet – a physical expression of our internal states. Also, with the latest discoveries in the quantum sciences, we are learning more and more about how all living organisms are in fact swathed in energy fields and waves of information flows. This realization of our hidden connections has been percolating through the corridors of human science as well as through our popular consciousness over the last few decades.

In coming together physically, through the external structures of our social networks and planetary communications, we are also coming together psychically as individuals around the world. In our diversity lies our unity: united through our connection, communication, consciousness and compassion. Already we are seeing the potentials when energetically connected individuals come together in the world today.

The Power of Energetically Connected Individuals

The fact that we are now increasingly connected around the planet means that we each have the potential to invest our individual energies as never before. And this is especially important for those people living outside the so-called 'privileged' societies. Whilst many may think that technological innovation is only available for developed nations, the reverse is true. Technological innovation has in fact had some of its most startling impacts in empowering poorer regions and peoples.

As mentioned previously, in the coming years there will be nearly 3 billion new minds coming online. The majority of these minds, voices and hearts will come from the developing nations as they connect to the planetary nervous system. They will be able to leapfrog over the need for an industrial revolution and jump directly into the digital age. Many people have failed to recognize the potential of the participation and input of the billions due to come online in the coming years from such cultures. After all, the human brain is an almost unlimited resource, unlike other resources on the planet. As the five billion poorer people become increasingly connected they will utilize global networks in ways the older generation will not be prepared for. It is likely that the future will be more defined by these 'poor peoples' than our current jet-setting crowd. When the future is open, networked and available for innovation, then it will be in the hands of those who can think out of the box or even without a box.

The game is already afoot in many ways, as we saw in the networked protests of the Arab Spring. Many regions and peoples that have suffered oppression and barbaric cultural restrictions will no longer tolerate these anachronistic ways of living. The new consciousness arising in these areas will also push forward new models that seek to override the incumbent status quo. The older power-orientated regimes will have a hard time trying to hold back the tidal wave of change demanded by the rising youth. As one commentator has referred to this situation – the 'desert' will want to have what the 'oasis' has . . . and they'll be ready to move out of the desert for it.[8] People are feeling the inherent inner potential to reach out, connect and be empowered. A single individual can energetically connect and catalyze thousands, if not millions, of other people within this new-paradigm era.

One example of this involves Oscar Morales, a resident of Columbia who one day felt so much anger against the FARC rebels[9] of his native country that he felt he had to express himself. That evening he created a Facebook page and named it Un Millón de Voces Contra Las FARC ('One million voices against FARC'). Morales created the group and made it public just after midnight on 4 January 2008. At 3 a.m. he went to bed. At 9 a.m. the next morning he woke up to check his group and found that 1,500 people had already joined. What was more astonishing was that by the late afternoon the same day the group had grown to include 4,000 members. By 6 January, the second full day, the group not only had 8,000 members, but people were actively posting on the discussion board and wishing to connect physically and publicly. In itself this event may not seem remarkable. However, the result is that on 4 February 2008 – a mere four weeks after the group was begun – millions of Colombians dressed in white marched throughout the country and in major cities worldwide to express their anger at FARC. Within a month one individual had managed to catalyze millions of people to come together in 27 cities in Colombia and 104 worldwide to march in empathy and solidarity. This is one example of the power of energetically connected individuals. We are seeing similar connected uprisings throughout the world.[10] However, these are early signs and may involve what I discussed earlier about being a frustrated part of the Bridge Generation. Yet those young individuals who will form part of the Phoenix Generation will not need to create conflict with existing systems, as they will create their own systems that will make the old models obsolete. As I have said, the young people today are born *into* change; whereas those that are to come will be born *as* change.

We do not necessarily need to connect with thousands of other people to share our energies. We can connect – and indeed are already connecting – in countless ways. In fact, each encounter we have with another person is an energetic exchange. George Kaponay, the originator of the EnergeticXChange concept,[11] and his family were travelling through South America on a journey to promote the values of energetic exchange when they bumped into a young Argentinian called Lugas in the jungle. Lugas had been travelling throughout South America without any money. When asked why he chose to travel like that Lugas replied that he had arrived in Chile with money, yet one day he happened to come across a very young girl, a child, in the street selling sweets for a living. There and then he decided to give her all his money. His reasoning was that if she could live on virtually nothing, then so could he. Lugas had been travelling since then on the kindness of strangers and the kindness of human 'energetic exchange'.[12]

Coming together involves a conscious understanding and appreciation of our connectivity as a diverse yet united species. Although we share information, it is much more than just the content we share. After all, information is not intelligence, and intelligence is not wisdom. Our networks (and governmental systems) can collect as much information as they wish. They can analyze as much data as they wish – yet data-collectors (whether humans or machines) are not necessarily intelligent. And if they be classed as intelligent, we cannot assume that they will be wise. True wisdom is the greatest resource we have on this planet, and the human being is the living essence that can act as an integral part of the dynamic intelligent whole.

Coming together as one involves our empathy, our humanity, our integrity and our ingenious capacity for innovation and creativity. In the next chapter I examine some of the creative innovation and new-paradigm models that are taking us into the future and toward the Phoenix Generation.

Chapter 7

New-Paradigm Values

Collaboration, not competition, is the royal road to the
wholeness that hallmarks healthy systems in the world.
Collaboration calls for empathy and solidarity, and
ultimately for love. I do not and cannot love myself if I do
not love you and others around me: we are part of the
same whole and so are part of each other.

Ervin László

A new paradigm is emerging in the opening decades of
the 21st century. The values that accompany this new
paradigm are pushing, prodding and nudging us to be
willing, open and receptive to ways of approaching
the emerging new situations. As our species is on the
cusp of forming a planetary society – an entangled web
of complex and multiple-level relations – we can no
longer work with industrial-era perspectives. We can
now see that the old hierarchical structures – where
information travels in linear paths from the top down
– are open to corruption, opacity and inefficiency. The
'public commons' of the past were closed down, which
led people to behave with less integrity in their dealings
with individuals and within their communities.

However, we have now entered the distributed era, of people collaboration, communication and networking. We are shifting from one set of C-Values: **Competition—Conflict—Control—Censorship** – to a new set: **Connection—Communication—Collaboration—Consciousness.**

To foster creative innovation the hierarchical model needs to shift toward ways of doing things that celebrate the collaborative community. The 'old energy' notion of secrecy must be replaced by one of sharing, which fosters integrity in human relations. Integrity in our human relations will inspire and motivate us to find solutions for our needs, and create innovative new ways and patterns of thinking. Such innovative and creative thinking is likely to be connected to the embrace of our diversity. After all, diversity recognizes the value of each individual mind, and allows each mind to connect with others around the world, and to share in the collective brainstorming. In this way, we can gradually shift from the 'ME-ness' of the industrial-era mindset toward the integrated-era value of 'WE-ness'. That is why I feel that as these years unfold we will see more and more people embracing an open-source culture that facilitates community sharing and development. In fact, it is happening already the world over . . . and the results are paradigm-breaking.

Open-Source Values

Open source is a philosophy and/or practice that promotes free access to all levels of information, whether it be in design, management, human resources or anything else. Open-source culture also requires trust in how individuals and communities share and develop their resources and ideas. In an age of distributed networks the way people and information connect must now move from a closed model to a collective, open, trust-based model that celebrates the joy of collaboration. Embracing the open-source culture will help to nurture transparency, truth and trust in our human and social relations. We can say that **Transparency** will generate flows of truth. **Truth** will generate trust between people. **Trust** will provide the engine for successful human collaboration, creativity, and inspired innovation. The way that many of us do things (whether as individuals, or in groups and organizations) now requires an open-source culture in which individuals are able to harness the distributed intelligence of the collective. It has been said that in a room full of experts, the greatest intelligence is to be found in the room, not in the individual experts.

There is wisdom within the crowd, as this old example illustrates. In 1906, Francis Galton, known for his work on statistics and heredity, came across a weight-judging contest at the West of England Fat Stock and Poultry Exhibition. An ox was on display and for sixpence fair-goers could attempt to guess the animal's weight after slaughter; the best guess would win the prize. Eight hundred people tried their luck, many of them having no knowledge of livestock. Galton hoped to prove the incapacity of the average voter and thought that this would be a perfect analogy for democracy. After the ox was slaughtered it weighed 1,198 pounds. Not one person came close to the final weight. However, when Galton averaged the guesses he discovered, to his complete surprise, that the result came to 1,197 pounds![1] In another, more recent example, author Harrison Owen relates a story of how he was asked to organize a conference for a large engineering company that had spent more than two years, and millions of dollars, designing an aircraft whose door would not work as planned. This open-source/open-space conference brought together everyone who had worked on the door from top managers and designers, down to everyone on the groundcrew, including even those who had done no more than touch the door. All compartmentalization of information was abandoned. The result was that the conference fixed the problem at negligible cost to the company. Results were achieved in a way that was not possible in traditional top-down management structures.[2]

Robert David Steele (a spokesperson for open-source culture) also notes how normal people, when they share information and collaborate, often arrive at better decisions than those made by so-called 'experts' under secret conditions. Steele's conclusion is that secrecy is a closed and ignorant energy, and he feels that the elimination of secrecy and top-down decision-making will be among the hallmarks of a new era. However, Steele also notes that the establishment of a transparent and 'open society' – one that is for 'We the People' – also requires the self-actualization of 'We the People.'[3] This is an important point; there can be no more than limited success if there is not a parallel development in the consciousness of the people involved. It is therefore timely now that we crack open the box on how we think, behave, work and relate to others. As we move into this new era of creative, connected minds we need to utilize the greatest asset we have – ourselves. The transitional bridge years, before the Phoenix Generation begins to rise, are about preparing the groundwork, and sowing the seeds in fertile soil. These emerging models are part of that groundwork and are being laid so that the future can be more transparent, trusting and truthful. This will be the energetic environment we need in order to respect, honour and empower people – irrespective of any artificial categories of class, status or anything else.

This innovative diversity has the potential to bring about a creative (r)evolution in our time by connecting people together to share with and catalyze one another – with an underlying design of unity. Our connected diversity has the ability to see problems and issues from new and often unexpected perspectives. Human innovation is set to have fewer constraints and less aversion to risk because not only are the old models failing us, but there is also greater necessity to try new things. We now have more incentive to be creative; and to try new, and often unknown, paths. As the poet Robert Frost so perceptively put it: 'I took the one [road] less traveled by | And that has made all the difference.'[4]

As more and more people contribute their ideas and envision the unexpected, this will undoubtedly inspire others to envision the previously thought impossible.

What is more, I fully expect to see more and more of the groundbreaking new ideas and visions coming not from the experts but from the non-specialists: the DIY enthusiasts and the backroom tinkerers. Such break-throughs from unexpected non-professional sources are what can be referred to as 'disruptive innovation'.[5] These are the people on the periphery – the non-traditionalists who go out on a limb to seek creative solutions from new perspectives. These 'disruptive innovators' will be made up of inspired young minds from all walks of life, from all social statuses, who will form a new era of young optimists who don't know what can't be done because they are plugged into the new era, not the old.

As we move through the transition years the structure of innovations will be dramatically altered. In the past many lone inventors and innovators were confined to their laboratories, or garages, feeling isolation from the greater community of like-minded pioneers. Often they were forced to seek funding from corporate sponsors or investors, who frequently restricted the distribution of their discoveries (or in some cases deliberately curtailed the development). What we are witnessing now is the formation of a network of 'distributed assistance', whereby projects and innovations are being open-sourced and finding eager helpers.

Distributed Assistance

It is my view that innovations will increasingly emerge through teams/groups of people working both locally and nonlocally on projects. They will pool their various skills, often connecting from diverse locations, and being less dependent upon centralized governmental or corporate funding. Such examples can already be found in such areas as community building/construction, finance, education and science.

i) Community Building

Marcin Jakubowski, a physicist turned farmer and inventor, founded the Open Source Ecology group in 2003 after he realized that the machines he needed to run his farm cost effectively did not exist. So he decided to design and build them himself, creating a 'Global Village Construction Set' (GVCS) with the aim of offering the means to construct vital machinery easily. Specifically, the Open Source Ecology group hopes to show how to fabricate fifty different industrial machines that are needed to build a small civilization with modern comforts. The blueprints for the construction set will be developed by people from various locations, before being built and tested on Jakubowski's farm. They will then eventually be distributed free of charge on the Internet. The Open Source Ecology group has attracted contributors from all over Europe and North America in the true open-source fashion. And yet Jakubowski had no formal training in the area of machine design and manufacture. This is one pioneering example of how innovative tinkerers – people with perhaps no traditional background in such areas – are moving into research and design. Innovation is entering from the periphery with little or no funding. Some are even funding themselves through the collaborative networks known as crowd-funding.

ii) Finance

Collaborative funding has really taken off in the last few years, with a whole array of projects – including films, music and technology – successfully finding funding from random individuals keen to invest and/or donate. In crowd-funding the person seeking the money makes a short video to present their proposal, and, often offers incentives for individual funders. Such incentives may range from being given the role of an extra in a film, or being first in line to benefit from the project when finished. This distributed model of funding actually empowers those involved (both funder and fund-seeker) as it allows them to be in a more direct relationship with how their money is used and where it goes. Furthermore, such arrangements are also usually much more transparent as the recipient of funds feels obligated to show how the funds are being used throughout the process from beginning to end. Using this financing model many projects can be supported, encouraged and successfully achieved outside of traditional financial industry pressures. Whereas crowd-funding is using the 'power of the many' to help spread the utility of money, the micro-finance model has also achieved success in empowering people.

Micro-finance has been especially beneficial in supporting local projects and businesses in poorer regions where it would have proven difficult to secure funds otherwise. Micro-finance is a means of supplying small loans to low-income people who traditionally lack access to financial services. It is a way of allowing many poorer people, with inspiring ideas, to help alleviate their poverty by starting new businesses and schemes. Modern micro-financing was largely revitalized by Muhammad Yunus's Grameen Bank of Bangladesh. It has now been joined by many other organizations – such as Kiva, Zidisha, Lend for Peace and the Microloan Foundation – that connect willing lenders to micro-entrepreneurs, many of whom live in some of the poorest regions of the world. Such micro-financing institutions have already given credit to more than 100 million borrowers. What this ultimately achieves is more people investing in their local region and communities, helping to alleviate the poverty of many under-represented people.

It seems to me that we are already beginning to understand, and implement, the concept of 'ecological economics'. These are schemes which support such practices as local currencies, bartering/exchange, and gift economies. One example of this 'distributed assistance' model that has been used to empower poorer people was the 'Equal Access' project which gained funding to place 7,000 satellite radio receivers into the poorest and remotest villages in Afghanistan to train teachers by broadcasting teacher-training programmes. Their pilot scheme trained over 3,500 teachers and benefited 150,000 students. Similarly, the Open BTS (Base Transceiver Station) is an open-source software/hardware combination that can offer mobile phone services through an open spectrum offering very low-cost communications. The project was started by Harvind Samra and David A. Burgess with the aim of drastically reducing the cost of mobile phone use in rural areas, especially in the developing world. This once again illustrates the new-paradigm values of offering low-cost, often free, distributed assistance the world over in a bid to alleviate radical disparities and to connect peoples and communities together.

The distributed assistance model also encourages a shift away from financial capital toward networks and relations that promote social capital. It is a model that encourages and strengthens relationships and collaborations, rather than ownership and property. The era we are moving into will promote values of access and collaboration, where sharing becomes the new 'ownership'. In other words, it will be a reverse of the older model of 'to gain in order to share', to 'to share in order to gain'. It is also especially about sharing and investing in the community. The emphasis will be upon supporting and investing in local people who have innovative ideas that can benefit their locality as well as the greater whole. The old model of centralized competition only favours the few to the detriment of the majority, and often bypasses communities and local well-being.

iii) Education

Human societies and cultures today are so much more complex than previously that the majority of educational institutions are ill equipped to play a positive role. The old pedagogic model is not only increasingly out of touch with the current world but also, more importantly, out of synch with any vision for the future. What is taught across our school systems is in danger not only of becoming increasingly archaic but also limiting, or even harmful, to a younger generation of emerging creative minds. We need to embrace the world that is to come, rather than 'training minds' for a world on the way out. As previously stated, the human mind is one of the greatest resources we have on this planet. We therefore need to nurture its development, rather than arrest its growth. Did you know that the ultimate computer in quickness, compatibility and efficiency has a petaflop of computing power, powered only by ten watts, and is about a litre in size? Yes – and it's called the human brain. Proper education, in line with the needs of its learners, is not only essential – it is a *necessity*. After all, who even teaches us how to think? Famed thinker Edward de Bono rightly asks why thinking isn't taught in our schools: 'Is it because thinking is not considered important? Is it because many people believe that thinking cannot be taught? Is this because we believe we are already teaching thinking?'[6] How we *think* is likely to undergo a shift in the years ahead as we move away from the enclosed classroom, surrounded by four brick walls, and enter a global space of learning.

Youngsters of today do not react to industrial-era style education methods of repetition and rote learning – they require dynamic multimedia communications that connect them across the world with their peers. This model of distributed peer-to-peer learning shifts the focus from the lone individual to the wider interdependent group. In this way the learning process ceases to be an isolated experience between an authority figure (the teacher) and a passive learner (the student). Learning is set to become transformed into a community experience. Education thus needs to shift into a collaborative model that utilizes both local and global networks to share knowledge and research. Technology and a globally connected world will converge to revolutionize education towards an online environment. This online revolution will broaden the reach of education and help to level the playing field for students from lower-income, less-privileged backgrounds.

We need to remind ourselves that when we talk about the younger generations we are also talking about the tens of millions of young minds being born into the poorer regions of the world. The 5 billion poorer people are likely to be among those who benefit most from open-source technology in education. For example, there are 10 million $35 tablet computers in India, and many educational establishments in India have already adopted open-source technology. India is not alone in working to educate its poorer citizens. Similarly, the One Laptop Per Child project (OLPC) aims to empower the world's poorest children through education. They have developed a rugged laptop (often referred to as the '$100 Laptop') that has been distributed to children in developing countries around the world. OLPC's mission is to provide young, poor children with the means to access knowledge, and opportunities to 'explore, experiment and express themselves'.[7]

Yet we should also be mindful that technology alone is not the answer. We also require our learners to develop a relationship with the natural environment. It is interesting that researcher Jeremy Rifkin notes how recent studies showed that children who during play-time were placed in artificial settings organized them-selves into social hierarchies whereas when placed in natural surroundings they organized themselves in more egalitarian relationships.[8] Rifkin foresees schools forging more relations with the environment, such as with park systems, wildlife organizations or environmental groups. I would agree that our younger generations, in line with an evolving consciousness, will seek a natural balance between virtual and physical (technological and environmental) relations.

At each epoch what we should be teaching is the consciousness of the era. In present terms this means reflecting the new-paradigm models of communication, collaboration and connectivity. This would then reflect the new-paradigm values of empathy and integrated systems. Moreover, integral consciousness is develop-ing alongside discoveries in the new sciences (quantum physics, neuroscience, biophysics and others), all of which reinforce the connected nature of the human self and its entanglement within the larger community of all living systems. How we connect and how we innovate is also influencing how we perform science.

iv) Science

Our connected diversity has the ability to see problems and issues from new and often unexpected perspectives. The way we think about tackling our global concerns is about to change. Science author Michael Nielsen describes how, for example, a mathematician in the Polymath Project decided to use his blog to tackle an unsolved mathematical problem. By collaborating with mathematicians from all over the world via the Internet the problem was solved in just 37 days. Nielson calls this 'networked science', and insists that this ongoing transformation of the way we collaborate in our projects and knowledge-base is rapidly speeding up the rate of scientific discovery.[9] Similarly, Nielsen refers to what he terms 'Citizen Science', in which amateur volunteers are connecting with the scientists of academia in problem-solving. This new wave of collaboration is successful, first of all, because of the Internet's ability to connect a wide range of distributed individuals and, secondly, because the diverse range of minds connecting across the planet increases the cognitive diversity active within the collaboration. As an example, Nielsen mentions how 250,000 amateur astronomers are working together in a project called Galaxy Zoo to understand the large-scale structure of the Universe, and how they are making astonishing discoveries, including an entirely new kind of galaxy. Such collaborations in science and innovation, between professionals and out-of-the-box amateurs, are increasing our combined brainpower and creative vision.

These emerging participatory and integrated models are set to stimulate new discovery and invention. With billions of creative minds set to join the global think-tank of the future there will be new thinking and new revelations over the coming years. We have to shift away from complaining about problems to solving them; then we can become a constructive part of our planetary social, cultural, environmental and conscious evolution. And as we think and do things differently, so will our values evolve over the coming generations.

New-Paradigm Obligations

The understanding of the integral relationship between each of us and our environment brings with it a renewed, shared responsibility. It is a vision of life that respects and honours our fundamental interdependence within living systems. Quality of life must be central to how we live; and also how we relate not only to family and friends but also to those we don't yet know. The imperative is on more fully developing our human communities and thus living more in balance with nature: human *being* means also human *belonging*. To do this we are required to make use of our technologies to live better, and live more sustainably.

Our shared fundamental values must embrace the inner world of the human, in harmony with focused and balanced social awareness. Many young people today are searching for a more satisfying and fulfilling social, intellectual, spiritual and emotional life. Those of us who have been born *into* change (rather than being born *as* change) are pulled between the need to contribute to our societies and the urge to seek for deeper insight into the meaning of life. The new-paradigm values ask from each of us that we are productive members of society, as we also strive to serve the greater humanity.

In a previous book that I co-authored with Ervin László,[10] we explored how the physical sciences will reflect our rising spiritual growth. In particular, that the new field-theory paradigm (what we referred to as the Akasha Paradigm), which explains our quantum entanglement, would help humanity in transcending its material differences to embrace our collective unity. We proposed that our new sciences would validate and corroborate a worldview that celebrated relationships, networks and connectivity, rather than supporting a conflicting paradigm of separation and competition. Further, that our new sciences are gradually portraying us as stewards of our environment rather than as conquistadors. This emerging worldview is the early birth of an integrating consciousness within humanity that reaches out to embrace our extended global family. Although this shift in perspective may be more difficult for older generations to adapt to, our younger and newer generations appear to understand integral consciousness almost immediately and without needing to intellectualize it.

As I have attempted to discuss in Part Two of this book, innovative changes in our social and technological systems are developing in parallel to a new era of social organization, communication and thinking patterns (or narratives). Humanity can be said to be empathically 'hard-wired' to evolve into a planetary civilization that celebrates diversity within unity. Our diversity is strengthened – not diluted – through our multiple connections and networks. Our unity is enhanced – not weakened – through our empathy, compassion and shared sense of responsibility and destiny. We are responding today to an unprecedented flow of energy, information and consciousness in our social, cultural and environmental surroundings. Such an intense range of impacts is inevitably catalyzing new patterns of thinking and ways of doing things. My feeling is that we are moving toward a restructuring of our inner psychological states as well as our external social structures. A new awareness in human consciousness is being birthed, and being driven through the heart of our social, economic and political systems. New organizational patterns are emerging, and with them new perceptions, understandings and worldviews. We are now being compelled to re-evaluate how we see ourselves not only within our local and global environments, but also in a grander, cosmological sense.

From this increased awareness and awakening will come a powerful urge to develop humanitarian, ecological and equitable systems. It often happens that an awakening in consciousness rouses the need to get involved in service for a common purpose. What we choose to do today will be inherited by the world to come. We each thus have an obligation to foster a more integrated, empathic and sustainable world. Our scope for sharing the new-paradigm values of **Connection– Communication–Collaboration–Consciousness– Compassion** has to be brought to bear on our future societies and our entire planetary civilization. We also require an individual human (r)evolution, a shift away from being absorbed in petty thoughts of a separate individuality and ego, to a recognition that as individuals we have an inherent connection with all life in the cosmos. The developmental awakening of each individual should be in balance with our daily life experiences – we do not need to retreat to a cave to seek self-development! Personal development becomes blocked if it does not embrace the individual as an aspect of the whole. We must therefore redefine – or refine – our own lives through this renewal of under-standing.

This period of (r)evolutionary change requires nothing less than a qualitative transformation in human consciousness. We do not need to wield physical or political power to be effective. Rather, we each can learn to expand and refine our ways of perception, thinking and action. The necessary transition toward a planetary society that is equitable and sustainable will only come through a (r)evolution in our consciousness. As Sri Aurobindo once wrote:

> Therefore the coming of a spiritual age must be preceded by the appearance of an increasing number of individuals who are no longer satisfied with the normal intellectual, vital and physical existence of man, but perceive that a greater

evolution is the real goal of humanity and attempt
to effect it in themselves, to lead others to it and
to make it the recognised goal of the race.[11]

Aspects of an evolving consciousness suggest
an empathic mind that is aware of its connectivity
both locally and globally, physically as well as non-
physically. It is time to view our situation through the
wide-angle lens of wisdom; we need to begin to see,
understand and act upon the bigger picture. We also
have to accept a psycho-spiritual growth within the
human race toward a shared, communal understanding.
This humanizing effect will encourage greater social/
community participation as well as pouring energy into
a planetary civilization. After all, whatever we each do
locally – with intention and energy – will be spread
around the world in countless unknowable ways. Our
sincere acts – our individual life of the spirit – must not
be subordinated to over-intellectualization or drowned
in the dogma of outward and empty forms of conduct
and mimicry. Everything we do, especially from now on,
must be real and genuine.

We have truly begun, for the first time in recorded
history, to birth a transcendent era – a quantum renaissance – in which transcendence becomes more central to
life. Not only is our well-being of paramount importance, as well as the well-being of all life on Earth, but
also central to life is the question of our evolutionary
imperative that drives us forward. We are about to see
a profound change in the presence of human life on
this planet.

There is a psycho-spiritual resonance emerging across the planet, energetically threading together each one of us. Now that we have the means to communicate and connect externally across time and space, our communal threads are responding to us and powerfully resonating our communality. However, these are signs of the beginning. The greater resonance is set to occur non-verbally as an inherent mindful awareness and an inner conscious knowing is birthed through our very cells/selves.

We are moving toward an era when change will not only be created externally, but will be born into humanity as part of our human biology. Our human biological nervous system – our quantum-state DNA – will *be* that change and give rise to a new form of intuitive human. We shall surely then see how incredible change can really be on our shared blue planet. This is set to be the era of our quantum renaissance – a time for the Phoenix Generation to usher in a burning new vision.

part three

THE PHOENIX GENERATION

Part Three offers an overarching perspective on what I have called the Phoenix Generation: the children being born in the second decade of the 21st century who will be in their teens around 2030. I believe that this unique generation will usher in a new evolutionary phase in humanity. The four chapters of this section discuss how the Phoenix Generation will be born with increased instinctive intelligence and with a greater degree of inherited wisdom. The chapters focus on how at birth the human quantum field calibrates with the Earth fields and how a different state of energy will affect the DNA of the baby and its growth. These chapters also explore how a form of quantum instinct and intelligence will give rise to changes in many diverse areas of social life, such as health, politics, education, well-being, self-actualization and cosmic awareness. The reality of a living, dynamic universe, complete with multidimensional aspects, will gradually emerge as the new mainstream perspective and worldview. A new epoch in the evolutionary development of humanity will have begun.

Chapter 8

The New Intuitive Human

I saw them cross the twilight of an age,
The sun-eyed children of a marvellous dawn . . .
The massive barrier-breakers of the world . . .
The architects of immortality . . .
Bodies made beautiful by the Spirit's light,
Carrying the magic word, the mystic fire,
Carrying the Dionysian cup of joy . . .

    Sri Aurobindo, Savitri

Social and cultural change is occurring fast on planet Earth. And it is set to unfold at an accelerating pace. Perhaps it is difficult for us to see this now as we are surrounded by a confusing array of impacts, fear-centred news and personal shocks. In Part One of this book I noted these concerns, and how important it is for those of us now living amidst these current impulses and influences to remain grounded and mentally–emotionally stable. In Part Two I noted how humanity has been undergoing a very notable psycho-spiritual evolution over the centuries – and especially recent decades – that is not immediately evident to many of us. Our modes of self-reflection and interest in transpersonal states have been preparatory stages in the fuller expression of human consciousness. I noted also how a global empathic mindset is emerging within humanity as we shift from one set of C-Values: **Competition–Conflict–Control–Censorship** – to a new set: **Connection–Communication–Consciousness–Compassion**. Within this transition we are also seeing how our social infrastructures and modes of human connectivity are moving from hierarchical structures to decentralized networks that connect people together directly. These new modes, established through our communication technologies, reflect the new expression of our collective human mindset. As stated earlier, these outward signs are the blueprints for a more subtle level of human interrelatedness. For now, this is our new vocabulary – the structures of how we must operate with conscious awareness until a time we can put aside such physical aids. In human terms it may seem that this development has been a long time coming. Within the bigger picture of evolutionary time, the process has been swift. In the last 150 years alone we have been witness to an amazingly rapid change.

The ebb and flow of human history has cradled the gradual unfolding of the individual, and the growing responsibility that this implies. This emerging 'blooming of the individual' has taken place alongside the story of the slow decline in aristocracy, elite rule and the demise of tyranny. The dismantling of hierarchical structures is required in order to make way for the rise of the aware and informed masses. This process has accelerated in recent centuries, with the fall of feudalism, the birth of democracy and the emergence of a connected global humanity. Alongside this we have also seen the increasing embrace and sharing of planetary values. We could say that human society is in the early contractions of planetary birth.

Conscious development is a psycho-spiritual process, aided by socio-cultural impulses and influences that have been woven throughout our history. Most recently, the strong impulses from the 20th century – and the 1960s in particular – have helped to catalyze the psychic environment and conscious awareness of many people the world over. Many seeds were planted that would germinate over time. The psychic states experimented with in the 1960s showed that there were alternative dimensions of consciousness, inspiring an eager young audience. The fall of the Berlin Wall in 1989, and the end of several archaic political institutions, gave a taste of the power for change when many thought it almost impossible.

Impulses of conscious renewal have been part of the ongoing process of human, cultural and psycho-spiritual evolution. True revolutions are not those of physical violence but of radical shifts in perceptions and knowledge, and ultimately in understanding of the human condition. The unfolding of the human journey has been expressed over the years through the expansion of intelligence, psychological awareness, humanitarianism, empathy and creative innovation. It has always been seen on the playing fields of the world – in stadiums and in streets the world over. For example, the instinctual nature of sport – its collaborative teamwork, its shared rules and game-play – can also be said to have played a role in the emergence of the intuitive human.

What I am suggesting in this chapter, and throughout this final section, is that, as global humanity shifts toward a planetary society, this will be matched by the rise of generations of conscious individuals who will *be the change*, rather than being *born into change*. Furthermore, the rise of individual intuition *inherent within each individual* will usher in new systems and ways of being. What I mean by this is that the age of big institutions ruling the game is coming to a close. The age of guru-hood, spiritual elitism, commercial 'teaching' methods and all the rest is going to be replaced by one depending on the interior spiritual insight (gnosis) in humanity. External frameworks of belief systems will gradually be replaced by a living intelligence – an intelligence that has always existed within the human race. When the truth is known instinctively, it no longer requires cultural preservation: no domes, spires, institutions or teachings. The living knowledge is more fluid and exists everywhere, for everyone, all of the time. We only need the means to access it. This way of access is a process that will unfold among human–planet–cosmos as these interrelated energetic environments alter their vibrational milieu. Over the unfolding years of this century each human will become their own 'teaching method' by their own *becoming* – humanity will be born increasingly connected to an inherent living intelligence. The old roles of central hierarchy will continue to diminish as humanity forms its own living biological network that connects each of us. In this decentralized manner, we are all of us critical to the whole: our connectivity and energy flows (physical, psychic, emotional) are no longer top-down but distributed. The days of a Messiah speaking to the multitudes are over. We are now moving into a time when it will be the multitudes that will amplify and spread the new energies.

The Phoenix Generation will represent this noticeable change, as these young minds and souls will be their own 'new teachers'. They will become the new politicians, financiers and business leaders, overturning the tables of the money-lenders. These creative forces will bring in new systems to replace the old, corrupt and inefficient systems that plague our societies today. In this way, they will serve to remove the obstructions and energy blockages that hold back humanity's emergence into a young planetary society. The main surge of the Phoenix Generation will be those born upon the Earth in these present years (2010–20), and who will be in their teens around 2030. The Phoenix Generation is here to accomplish what the current generation has only just begun. This is my speculation and understanding for the future.

Yet before the Phoenix Generation there were already forerunners arriving upon our terrestrial shores.

Portents of the New Human

We have always had unusual geniuses appearing here and there within human society. World-famous names fill our artistic rosters – child prodigies in music, art or mathematics. We have always preferred to consider such creative anomalies as 'geniuses' as it is a comfortable label. Another category that society has labelled as an extraordinary anomaly is that of the 'savant' (from the French *savoir* 'to know'). The savant – sometimes pejoratively called the 'idiot savant' – is a person who, whilst exhibiting mental disabilities, also demonstrates profound and extraordinary capacities. Such capacities are not only astounding but also far in excess of what we would consider to be normal abilities. Examples include being able to tell which date Easter will fall on 10,000 years into the future; having incredible memories that can recall statistics like a computer; or having a mathematical brain capable of computing numbers in the quintillion that even computers are unable to sequence. It has been claimed that during the Second World War, the British employed two mathematical savants to serve as human computers for 'unbreakable' codes.[1] And yet most of these same savants have incredibly limited conversational vocabulary and at times almost non-existent social skills. Furthermore, such people may be unable to provide themselves with the stimulus needed to use their abilities, and respond only when questioned by another person.

In such cases it seems improbable that these savants are able to acquire such information from available sources. So this begs the question – from where do they pull their answers? It is interesting to note that many savants are considered to suffer from a neuro-developmental disorder, an impairment in the brain or central nervous system. The neuronal network of the human brain and the central nervous system are key receptors in accessing both biological and environmental electromagnetic fields. Perhaps it is the case that impairment in 'normal' development has left some people with the 'dysfunctional ability' of accessing greater fields of living information that are usually shielded to 'normal', socially conditioned individuals. However, regardless of the speculations here, we still have to acknowledge that savants are not balanced individuals in the sense of being able consciously to apply their capacities coherently within human societies. Rather, they are examples of certain capacities manifesting and operating in disequilibrium. Yet such potentials are surely portents of what capacities lie in wait within the human being. Whilst savants are known to be born with their abilities, there have been many instances of other ways in which people have suddenly been propelled into unusual and perhaps future-orientated evolutionary traits. Some of these instances have been documented as accidental near-death experiences (NDEs).

NDE researcher P M H Atwater has worked specifically with children who have undergone such experiences at a young age. She reports that young near-death 'experiencers' are impacted by a range of physiological and psychological after-effects that appear to make alterations both in the brain and in the nervous system. The result of this is that many such young children have sudden 'awakenings' to things of a sacred and spiritual nature.[2] Yet rather than being due to some sort

133

of ephemeral effect, Atwater notes that the emergence of psychic abilities that occurs after many such NDEs is related 'directly to perceptual enlargements of the electromagnetic range and to extensions of faculties normal to us'.[3]

Atwater cites an unusual array of real-life cases of young children who have had near-death experiences, and their resulting changes. This includes Carrol Cray[4] (experiencer of five NDEs) who by two and a half could read and write, had a library card, and was reading the newspaper. L S Gordon (NDE at age three during tonsillectomy), who could read and understand physics when ten, also studied world religions and spiritual practices at an early age. Gordon considered our consensus reality to be a 'Scotch-tape-and-cardboard affair' (his words); and exhibited a high IQ despite hating school. William (NDE at two months, suffocated by falling chair) exhibits the ability to see all sides of an object at once; has full-blown synaesthesia (multiple sensing); is gifted in languages; and is self-taught in computers. Similarly, Lynn (NDE at 13 during open-heart surgery) began to display feats of psychokinesis once she returned home. This included seeing images whenever she touched objects (synaesthesia); knowing who owned an object by just touching it (psychometry); and seeing a person's life in flashes, including their future (clairvoyance). Finally, Flavio – whose mother had an NDE – likewise exhibits psychic abilities and calls himself a 'cosmic messenger' who is here to speak about spiritual matters as a bridge between worlds. He has said that,

> Now that this world is starting to be less physical,
> other children like me are going to come ...
> Human beings are different now. They are going
> to be more open. I am here to calm people who
> are frightened by the changing energy of Earth.[5]

Before Flavio was a teenager he wrote the book *Vengo del Sol* (*I Come from the Sun*), which became a bestseller in his native Argentina. Atwater summarizes these unusual results by saying that 'The child you get back after a near-death episode is a remodeled, rewired, reconfigured, refined version of the original.'[6]

In a similar manner psychologist Kenneth Ring, who has studied NDEs for nearly 40 years, has concluded that such experiences appear to accelerate a psycho-physical transformation. Ring believes that such encounters may well herald what he calls the 'shamanizing of modern humanity' in that they are part of the preparation for helping to develop humanity's latent capacities for a direct, intuitive mode of perception.[7] Ring uses the word 'Edglings' to describe such people, especially younger children, who through such experiences may be closer to a higher form of human development than most of us. Another NDE researcher, Margot Grey, found that many people returned from the experience with a changed worldview. Such people tended to perceive the universe as a living intelligence, with an understanding of the primacy of consciousness. Likewise, Ring's study groups almost all tended to agree that their experiences reflected a purposive intelligence and that they were part of an accelerating evolutionary current that is driving humanity toward higher consciousness. Both Ring and Grey concluded that such excursions into what they refer to as the 'nonlocal realm' appeared to offer access to a triggering mechanism that somehow results in a biologically based transformation of the human self.[8]

Ring and Grey both believe that having an extraordinary experience with a nonlocal connectedness actually impacts the human nervous system, possibly releasing transformative energy, or at least in some form affecting the biological system of the individual. They view people who have experienced the nonlocal realm, whether through NDEs or by other methods, as being the forerunners of a new species of humanity. Both agree that the real significance of such nonlocal encounters may actually be in their 'evolutionary implications for humanity'.

This hypothesis is extremely interesting when we consider it in the light of current global 'nonlocal' communication networks that offer an alternative version of transcending the time–space nexus of physical reality. Our young children are being born into a world where on a daily basis – 24/7 – human consciousness flows through millions upon millions of computers, networks and web devices, forming a nonlocal realm of information and living intelligence. And it is not just in virtual space; this also occurs through countless movies, books (like this one!), articles, songs, videos and more. A field of connectivity transcends our old temporal and spatial boundaries. Our human information technologies increasingly mirror – and reflect – the living field of intelligence that grows ceaselessly upon the Earth. It is my understanding that such a web is the external reflection of our own inherent, non-visible connectivity. My view is that recently developed forms of nonlocal connectivity have a tangible impact upon the human neuronal system. These impacts – such as stimulating human empathy – also catalyze some release of transformative energy. There is no external model of communication and connectivity that does not have its corresponding reality in human consciousness. These impacts upon the human most likely also cause changes within DNA, which I have referred to in Chapter 6 as a biofield in a state of quantum coherence. These changing DNA vibrational patterns not only take effect intragenerationally but also between generations. That is why the Phoenix Generation being born into this world will be unlike any previous generation of children (*see* Chapter 9). According to Atwater some of the attributes attached to the current generation of children (born prior to 2002) include being supersensitive, confident, highly intelligent, creative, non-conformist, psychic and spiritually aware, impatient, empathic, good at problem solving, and difficult to educate. Similarly, they exhibit higher intuition, mental and technological abilities; show hypersensitivity to field effects; have a strong curiosity to learn; are more sensitive to crowds and group energies; and are highly intuitive.[9] Can we imagine how these traits will develop in successive generations?

As far back as 1999, when the book *The Indigo Children* was first published, it opened the lid on a new phenomenon that suggested humanity was witnessing the beginnings of a consciousness shift through a new generation of young children. These young minds were said to be the new-paradigm forerunners set to herald a change in the human lineage. Unfortunately, much mis-information has sprung up since concerning the subject of 'Indigo' children. The most widespread misleading claim is that all 'Indigos' are super-psychic children; some with glowing auras who exhibit unique gifts of clairvoyance, healing and so on. Some claims even go so far as to say that they are all incarnated space children being born now to help save the world. Such names as Star Children, Crystal Children, and Rainbow Children are being cashed in and promoted, with centres popping up, and books being hastily written, to help parents and children come to terms with their supposedly new abilities.

Yet how did these children come to be labelled as the Indigos in the first place? Well, the story begins with a woman called Nancy Ann Tappe, who has a neurological condition known as synaesthesia, which means that her brain cross-wires two senses and the result, in her case, is that she is able to 'see' people as colours. This is different from the psychic ability to view auras. In Tappe's case it was simply that her brain picked up colours from people according to their categories of behaviour. After monitoring this for a number of years, Tappe was able to intuit a person's character and way of being from the colour she 'saw' associated with them.

Then something happened – she began to see a 'new colour' coming into the world. Interestingly, this new colour was only appearing around children. It was an indigo-blue colour that, for Tappe, represented a new kind of person being born on the planet. What this suggested was that the new generations were coming into the world with a slightly different range of feelings, behaviour and thinking. In other words, children were being born with a different state of energetic presence. However, in the end it is not about names, nor is it about trying to be different. The bottom line is that it seems new generations of children are exhibiting a different form of consciousness, set of attitudes and perceptions about the world. For example, whilst many of the older generations grew up trusting and abiding by authority, without much questioning, the younger generations are finding themselves at odds with the system. To many of the younger minds our current systems seem crazy and illogical. Naturally, they wish to express themselves and to question incumbent authority. It is a question of value systems, and many antiquated values are making it difficult for the younger generations to fit in with our obsolete programming and mindsets. According to Tappe (in 2009), 97% of children under the age of 10 are Indigos, and 60% of the children older than 15 are as well.[10] Lee Carroll, co-author of the original book *The Indigo Children*, noted that 10 years after publishing the first book it is finally being acknowledged that 'today's children represent an evolution of the human species.'[11] Many of our younger children today are literally rewired and eager to make creative contributions to a world they perceive as being topsy-turvy. We are seeing such contributions already from young children on YouTube making speeches against our inefficient systems. One example from many is the case of Victoria Grant who, at the age of 12, spoke at the 'Public Banking in America Conference' (27 April 2012; Philadelphia, PA) on why her homeland, Canada, and most of the world, is in debt and what should be done about it.[12] The children and young adults of today are beginning to break the old patterns and become the early wave of pioneers and system-busters. They are showing a remarkable intuitive grasp of our modern technologies. They are reaching out and connecting; forming networks; returning to ecological themes; supporting alternative health practices; forming community projects; praising local food; re-invigorating a sense of the sacred; and pushing out the boundaries for new thinking. It is not occurring everywhere, or with everyone. There is still much confusion and emotional angst in our younger generations. However, a more intuitive human is coming through.

The Emperor Finally Has No Clothes

A different conscious energy is emerging in the early decades of the 21st century that will continue to unfold within humanity's newborns. As distinct from the rational linear phase, an integrated field-type consciousness is rising that no longer tolerates the old-paradigm structures of separatism, egoism and materialism. Rather than being a full-frontal revolt against incumbent systems, a wave of reformist change will arise from the subtlety of this new human energy. Arising will be a new generation of young people driven to contribute to constructive social change and indifferent to the old hierarchical structures of control and power. Part of the reformist change will be the increase in transparency in our social systems. It is already happening now – we are seeing increased instances of corruption (political, financial or personal) coming to the surface and being exposed. As the sun rises, they say, the shadows will at first become sharper and more visible; the inadequacies and ineffectual systems will increasingly be exposed. That which was hidden in the labyrinth of social illusion and wordplay will simply become revealed – in the hope that it might be healed and/or replaced. Those institutions, practices and societies built upon fear and disingenuous values will falter as a new pattern of human thinking/ feeling/sensing responds to changing values and modes of integration. Soon, even our youngest babes will be pointing at the old idols and declaring, open-mouthed: 'But look, they are not wearing any clothes!' At that point, edifices and traditions will be forced either to disintegrate or renew/recalibrate according to the new patterns.

The protective veneer of social appearance, status and so on, that once held sanctuary for certain people, will no longer operate. Celebrities, politicians, wealthy elites, religious leaders, once-respected public figures – the façade will drop from many such people and the wave of transparency will make visible their misdemeanours. So much dirty laundry will be washed in public as a generation of instinctually driven young minds and hearts will wish to heal a planet in order to create and reform anew. Those of the Phoenix Generation will be guided instinctively by the currents of living information. The scarcity we have hitherto felt has not been in physical resources but in vision and imagination. This lack will be more than made up for as creative and inspiring minds connect around the world, as well as within to an inner source of trust and confidence. In this way the early tremors of youth insecurity (witnessed in violent outbursts and psychological instability) will be increasingly replaced by a form of internal guidance as the human instinct once again becomes the principal force within human action. Many of us are already becoming students to our children and to the young adults in the world. We have witnessed how unquestioning faith in external sources of information, opinions and authority is challenged by these young minds. The emerging intuitive human wishes to step away from the conditioning structures of external dogma. Belief systems will hold less meaning for the Phoenix Generation as they realize that these external, linguistic and ideologically based structures are limiting to the self and take away the individual's responsibility for their own self-empowerment.

The Phoenix Generation will be operating more in the flow of common sense – yet it will be a different 'common sense' from that which we are accustomed to. A common sense that is neither 'common' nor makes 'sense' to us now will originate from a different state of awareness. Human behaviour that made sense for when we imagined we lived as islands of individuality will no longer 'make sense' – nor be functional – for a species that consciously experiences the interconnectivity of all life. The more the human species transforms internally the greater the change we will see occurring in our physical world – in our societies, technologies, culture and more. The next generation cannot be the same as the present, or the previous. In this moment of human history to give birth to a duplicate generation – with the same ideals and values – would result not in a perpetuation of human societies but in their demise. That is why we need transformational change in the very psycho-spiritual orientation both inter- and intra-generationally. For those of us now in the world – the Bridge Generation – it has taken consistent exertion and energies to override external constraints upon our inner guidance systems. We have struggled against the onslaught of various social conditionings that have hindered – or blocked – the flows of inner perception. Now, change will come more easily and more rapidly.

The changes that the Phoenix Generation will usher in during the years ahead (*see* Chapter 10) will be more profound than the changes that took place during our industrial revolutions. This period of our industrialization transpired over more than a century – the changes that will occur with the Phoenix Generation will emerge in the span of just a single human lifetime. We will see in action that communication, transparency, and honesty are much more powerful tools than secrecy, fear and confrontation. Not only will the instinctive human communicate with past 'enemies', but they will share the same hopes and dreams. The emperor's falsely polished suit of body armour will disintegrate in the face of transparent, honest eyes. The sham elements within our political, financial, corporate and media structures will scramble to maintain their façade; yet will have no hope of doing so in the minds and hearts of a generation connecting with a living source of information – their inner truths. Our current archaic educational structures will no longer be able to force students to adopt and comply with outdated structures of thought. With or without us, the new young minds will create their own freedom to inspire and renew their world into being. By this stage they will possess a vast inner world, connected to a planetary network of information, contacts and friends. Fearful incumbent structures of authority will attempt to control such technologies of communication,[13] yet they will ultimately fail against the inevitable tide of evolutionary awakening.

The Phoenix Generation will likely be the ones to free humanity from the dominance of erroneous ideas – ideas that forged war, created poverty and hunger, and sustained dis-ease. We are giving birth to a generation that will be successful in removing these illusions from the field of human consciousness. The new intuitive human has been in the making for some time now. Our world is far more peaceful today than it has been at any time – despite what our controlled mainstream media may be saying. This signals to us that the emotional frequency of the Earth is changing, encouraging people to seek peaceful solutions wherever possible. The living intelligence that is a part of the human instinct is also a spiritual, empathic and nurturing intelligence, which has been lacking in much of modern human awareness. This living intelligence is also a loving intelligence. The masculine energy of intelligent love will be stepping back in order to allow the rise of the feminine energy of loving intelligence.

Those of the Phoenix Generation will usher in a period when the feminine and masculine energies of the world will be rebalanced. Values of love, compassion, understanding, patience, tolerance and empathy will be more openly expressed and part of an active world – and not seen as predominantly 'female' values. The division that separates the masculine and feminine energies will dissolve, and be replaced by a newer energy of unity – of coming together. Similarly, the artificial stigma around 'male' and 'female' roles in the world will be changed through the younger 'phoenix' men and women re-modelling role expectations. Women will be more keenly appreciated, sought and brought into collaboration in such major areas as global politics, the economy and business. An all-round intuitive energy will be the marker for the upcoming decades, and will find expression by young women of the Phoenix Generation holding key positions as change agents. Although some people are speaking about the rise of the 'new divine feminine', I would suggest that what is actually set to occur is a long overdue rebalancing of the male and female energies. We are moving toward an era of human evolution in which integrated energies – energies of coherence and harmony

– will be established as the principal energies. The notion of one side having dominance over the other (whether male *or* female) is an old energy. Let us remember that the old energy divided and polarized, and was based on duality. The newer energies are focused on balance and bringing everything together into an integrated whole that respects diversity within unity.

Now, in the early decades of the 21st century, humanity is poised upon the cusp of a transition for which evolution has long been preparing. And the pace of preparatory change grows exponentially with each passing year. The energies are also spreading from human to human through our biofields, and upon the electromagnetic epidermis of the Earth. Soon there will not be an area isolated from such influence, as each village and town will have in its midst a new intuitive human – more so when the Phoenix Generation rise upon the Earth and begin to take up their social positions.

There is something immensely exciting happening here on this planet. Something is rising within us, amongst us and through us, and penetrating the very fabric of the Earth. It is a transformation without words, passing through each and every individual. It seems that part of our 'internal equipment' as human beings is our inbuilt ability to activate latent capacities in alignment with evolutionary requirements. Our next alignment, it appears, is through DNA and the human nervous system.

Chapter 9

Our Energetic Resonance

The true change of consciousness is that which will change
the PHYSICAL conditions of the world and will make of it
an entirely new creation.

The Mother (Mirra Alfassa)

Psychologists and evolutionary biologists alike have
noted that, thanks to our evolutionary history, we have
a background in an 'us vs. them' attitude to our world.
This confrontational behaviour is a survival from our
historical past that we have brought with us into our
present-day world. Such rudimentary behavioural traits
have also spilled over into the everyday values that have
served to divide the world into sets of us and them. For
millennia these divisions have been reflected in politics,
education, national and international conflicts, and in
the general way we sought to 'conquer' dear planet Earth.
Such traits cannot remain with us for much longer, as
they neither serve the people nor the future of the planet.
Let me explain further the relationship between the Earth
and its inhabitants.

In relating human biology to the Earth it is interesting
to note that due to the large size of the human baby's

head at birth modern humans are born 'premature' in the evolutionary sense.[1] The baby's head is thus not fully developed at birth, and for this reason human babies require more parental care time than other animals before being able to be self-sufficient. What this means is that humans are predisposed to develop more fully within the Earth's magnetic/energy environment. We are pushed out early so that our nervous systems can acclimatize to and resonate with the resident Earth frequencies.

Much of our human growth occurs after birth when we are in a social environment. In the past this has made the human being overly susceptible to the social conditioning that arrives through various external impacts to build up layers of acquired knowledge. Thus, a child's understanding of the world she inhabits is more or less an artificial construct aligned with the specific social consensus of the time and place. The early imaginative shoots of a child's creative reality-formation are usually cut down short in order to trim the child's perceptions in line with the dominant paradigm. This harsh act of social programming serves to push a young child's natural instinctual intelligence to the background, replacing it with an ego-based social persona. Then the slow process of institutional teaching begins, with years of classroom rote-learning and forced memorization of fixed ideas. Why are we so inept at birth that we need almost one and a half decades of legalized learning before we are deemed fit to be released into the wide 'wild' world?

Interestingly, this is not the case, relatively speaking, with the animal kingdom. Many baby animals are born with a high degree of pre-wired instinctual intelligence that provides them with the necessary survival skills alongside minimal parental care. Part of this in-built intelligence comes from inherited wisdom which is passed on genetically through the species.[2] It is my premise that the Phoenix Generation will show increased intuitiveness and instinctual intelligence similar to the animal kingdom as their nervous systems will be fine-tuning to a modified Earth frequency. In this manner, such children will not have to be taught everything from scratch in cloistered classrooms. Instead, they will exhibit rapid learning traits as if they appear to 'get' concepts much quicker – in some cases almost immediately. It will seem as if they are just more tuned in to what is going on.

So just what is going on?

At birth the human quantum field (via human DNA) connects and calibrates with the Earth's own frequency patterns. A different energy signature on the Earth will therefore affect the DNA resonance of the baby and its growth. What I am positing here is a *DNA Frequency–Earth Alignment* – an entrainment process that involves the calibration of Earth energy with human DNA upon birth. We could refer to this as a form of *quantum instinct and intelligence*. Now back to the quantum details, some of which were touched upon previously.

Research findings in biophysics note that DNA has a liquid crystal lattice-type structure which emits biophotons.[3] Through the light-emitting process DNA produces a field-organizing effect that overlaps, forming what is called inductance.[4] Induction is a process that we are very familiar with in physical systems, yet now we are coming to realize that it also operates through DNA and the human body. This induction then amplifies the signal through the creation of a form of coherence – what I referred to in Chapter 6 as quantum coherence. This state of coherence allows for a form of instant communication to occur as each of the 100 trillion molecules in the body has its own magnetic field, each one overlapping with the next. DNA thus creates an electromagnetic pattern as its molecules resonate in sync. This synchronization allows for biological information within the body to be processed simultaneously. The field-like properties of DNA therefore cause the human body to act as a giant transformer, or like an antenna receiving/ broadcasting signals. It is for this reason that some people are concerned that the rise in electromagnetic pollution is having a tangible negative effect upon human health.[5]

In light of these recent findings we can refer to DNA as being *quantum DNA*. That is, DNA not only operates in a linear fashion to encode genetic information and protein building, but it also emits a nonlocal energy field. It is within this field that instantaneous communication can occur through a coherent pattern of waves at the quantum level. This suggests that the 97% of human DNA that is not involved in protein building is active within a quantum state. It may well be that increased manifestations of field-like, nonlocal forms of intuition and knowing (what may be termed speculatively as *quantum consciousness*) will come from part-activation of the portion of DNA that so far has baffled our scientists as to its function. With trillions of overlapping DNA fields – each with a mini electromagnetic field – creating a whole biofield, we experience a unified human consciousness. Furthermore, human consciousness comes with an energy (magnetic) imprint, or signature. Such a potential activation of our quantum DNA may relate to a future state of human consciousness that has until now remained largely dormant. The activation of such dormant capacities within human DNA may result from evolutionary necessities. It could be the case that until now humanity has not been sufficiently prepared for its activation. According to one well-placed commentator on metaphysics:

> The human being's organism is producing a new complex of organs in response to such a need. In this age of the transcending of time and space, the complex of organs is concerned with the transcending of time and space. What ordinary people regard as sporadic and occasional bursts of telepathic or prophetic power are . . . nothing less than the first stirrings of these same organs.[6]

As the revered Persian poet Rumi also writes, 'New organs of perception come into being as a result of necessity | Therefore, O man, increase your necessity, so that you may increase your perception.'[7]

This transcendental stage of consciousness, depicted above as being a part of our natural evolutionary heritage, is connected with the human brain and nervous system. We now know that we have a DNA quantum field activated within our bodies. This quantum informational

151

field throughout the human body will determine the coherence of our biofields. And human biofields – and thus human consciousness – are affected by various external impacts: environmental, cultural and cosmic. In other words, the human nervous system responds to fluctuations in the electromagnetic frequencies caused by terrestrial, solar and cosmic sources. As the frequency waves of various terrestrial and cosmic forces – gravitational, magnetic, plasma, and others – fluctuate this will result in a different set of wave patterns (vibrations) entering the human quantum DNA field. Such vibrational impacts/influences have the potential to be a significant driver in catalyzing an increased conscious awareness in humanity.

The result from an increased activation of 'quantum conscious coherence' would also likely lead to increased intuitive faculties and the rise of extrasensory phenomena. The rise of these attributes within a percentage of the Phoenix Generation could eventually lead to a critical mass that would tip human consciousness into new modes of perception in successive generations. This 'incredible information' is part of the new understanding emerging from the latest findings in quantum science, and which creates for us a different view of how our reality is constructed.

It is not surprising to learn that humanity has all but lost its connection to the quantum world, exacerbated in recent centuries by the dominant material, rational and linear paradigm. Flashes of 'quantum-connection' from the past became relegated to the world of myth, folklore and fantastical supernatural stories. The quantum world does not fit into such a rationalistic perception – it does not succumb to a 'clockwork universe'. However, modern sciences are once again validating the ancient 'spiritual' traditions that taught of an entangled universe. Soon this will lead us to comprehend the presence of multi-dimensional reality. It is highly likely that the young minds of the Phoenix Generation will instinctively sense and relate to a field-view of reality.

An Informational Field-View of Reality

The evolutionary development of a *quantum conscious-ness* within humanity could form the basis for the collective mind of the species. The latest findings in the quantum sciences – notably quantum mechanics and biophysics – posit a field-view of reality that is likely to underpin the next stage in human evolution. Various mystics and consciousness researchers have alluded to this by a variety of names in the past – cosmic conscious-ness, superconsciousness, transpersonal consciousness, integral consciousness and so on. All these descriptions share a common theme, namely the rise of intuition, empathy, greater connectivity to the world and to people, and a sense of 'inner knowing' (gnosis). Further, the emergence of a form of *quantum consciousness* would likely catalyze an awareness of cosmic humanism, the realization that humanity exists and evolves within a universe of intelligence and meaning. This would serve to seed within humanity a more profound, non-dogmatic spiritual impulse.

Forms and intimations of these new consciousness patterns are already emerging in the world, but as yet they have not become a part of our accepted paradigm. Earlier evolutionary 'conscious mutations', for example, included visionaries, mystics, artists, psychics, and a smattering of young children (such as the 'Indigo Children').

As Dr Richard Bucke stated in his work *Cosmic Consciousness*, the early signs of this new evolutionary development have been appearing within humankind for some time:

> The simple truth is, that there has lived on the earth, 'appearing at intervals', for thousands of years among ordinary men, the first faint beginnings of another race . . . This new race is in the act of being born from us, and in the near future it will occupy and possess the earth.[8]

I would posit that social and cultural events have occurred throughout world history that have served to seed higher functioning into human consciousness. Such events have taken the form of artistic movements, scientific innovations, faith movements, cultural/social revolutions, architecture, fraternities, myths and legends, sporting fixtures, and more. All such socio-cultural impacts affect the field of human consciousness in a way that prepares the human mind for periods of development and change. Within these seemingly random occurrences lie the components that act as the 'technologies' for our development. I would suggest that the last few centuries of human history, in particular, have seen the rapid expansion of our informational flows, and thus human awareness in general.

The increasing development of what we term human 'collective consciousness' is most likely to be in line with certain evolutionary necessities. Within this development lie the catalysts for stimulating capacities within the human being that have largely lain dormant in the majority of humankind. Preparation has been necessary through a succession of events that overall form a pattern of mutually reinforcing stimuli aimed at raising humanity's psychic awareness. This includes the expansion of intellect, psychological awareness, social development, humanitarianism, empathy and creativity. These developments, I suggest, have also resulted in stimulating the intuitive connection between our inner and outer realities. In other words, there have been moments throughout recent human history that helped prepare the 'mental soil' for a new consciousness slowly to seed and grow. Yet this is nothing new as throughout history there have been individuals, feeling the presence of evolutionary change, who have been caught up in social-cultural upheavals. These events and human efforts, according to Gopi Krishna, indicate a stirring of the human evolutionary impulse:

> I can safely assert that the progress made by mankind in any direction, from the subhuman level to the present, has been far less due to man's own efforts than to the activity of the evolutionary forces at work within him. Every incentive to invention, discovery, aesthetics, and

the development of improved social and political organizations invariably comes from within, from the depths of his consciousness by the grace of ... the superintelligent Evolutionary Force in human beings.[9]

I would further add here that in order for continued human development to occur there are particular periods of human history wherein humanity becomes ready, or in need of, the activation of particular faculties or evolutionary traits. During such transitional periods humanity will acquire – or be coerced into developing – new capacities of consciousness and awareness. As in all paradigm shifts, old energies must inevitably give way to the new – as represented by the incoming Phoenix Generation. As one thinker has stated:

> We live in changing times whereby humanity is undergoing a transformation. Our consciousness, which has a vast potential for further development, must undergo a release from old, binding structures, and break out towards a rapid expansion . . . We need to understand phenomena at deeper levels, and not just accept what we are told, or what is fed to us through well-structured social institutions and channels. We must learn to accept that our thinking is a great tangible spiritual force for change.[10]

In the years ahead a new breed of young hearts and minds will be manifesting a consciousness that is both open to spiritual impulses and simultaneously aware and attentive to the latest in scientific research. A new generation will be growing up aiming for a collective sense of well-being, connectedness, empathy and creative vision.

It is possible that a newly activated quantum state/ capacity within the human being will open up access to an unimaginable energy field of information. This would then lead to new vistas of creative intelligence that would allow a young humanity to usher in new models and ways of being to make our incumbent, inefficient systems obsolete (*see* Chapter 10). Such access to nonlocal fields of intelligence will not come about as some grand televised 'Eureka moment' but rather as the gradual unfolding of inherent human capacity. In time such human capacity will become commonplace and normal. At first, however, it is expected to emerge as instinctual intelligence within the new human. This is a natural organic shift as the quantum field of human DNA, in resonance with nonlocal information– energy fields, becomes a stronger route to access human consciousness. When human physiology is tuned into a direct interaction with nonlocal energy fields then we are more likely to perceive non-ordinary states of consciousness. Therefore, through our nonlocal field connectedness we can begin to acclimatize ourselves to accepting information/feelings through what we might have previously labelled as the sixth sense. The concept of nonlocality to the physicist is the same as what the mystics used to refer to as holistic interconnectedness.

The experience of direct nonlocal consciousness used to be the domain of adept practitioners (shamans, mystics, psychics) who would have undergone rigorous and lengthy training. Our everyday mindset of the local view of the universe is largely unprepared for the realms of non-ordinary reality. In our present era, and in Western civilization especially, the nonlocal mode of perception (subjective experience) has not been encouraged, or even recognized. It has lain dormant, atrophied and become the province of the esoteric sciences. The rationalist view of reality has established the dominating values of competition, power, ego and greed. A nonlocal, intuitive sense of reality, however, will be one that embraces the new-paradigm core values of **Connection–Communication–Consciousness–Compassion**. It is my view that the Phoenix Generation will be the first generation of youngsters to embody these values in a widespread manner – thus ushering in a new epoch for the development of human consciousness. This awakening has already begun as the human being opens up in resonance to the flows of living information.

Connected to Living Information

It appears that the Earth is now receiving different forms of energetic impacts – especially electromagnetically – which will alter its resonant energy signature. As I discussed in a previous book,[11] Earth's magnetic field is showing signs of large cracks (some the size of California), making the planet increasingly open to solar winds and coronal mass ejections (Sun flares). The Earth's magnetic field is not a static shield, but rather like an oscillating wave, and fluctuations in the field are known to affect living systems upon the Earth. Biological bodies, being electrical energy units, are sensitive to external energetic and atmospheric variations – though usually these reactions operate at a subconscious level. Likewise, magnetic variations can have unusual effects on human thought processes. One example is the impact of magnetic fluctuations upon human short-term memory as memory processes are tied into the electrical (that is, magnetic) functioning of the human nervous system. Our sciences are now understanding more and more how human life – our thoughts, emotions and behaviour – is affected directly by fluctuations in Earth's magnetic field. The breach in Earth's magnetosphere, which is its natural protective shield, is allowing large volumes of solar radiation to enter the atmosphere. Not only will this increase the impact of solar storms on our physical infrastructure (for example, the global telecommunications networks), but it can also significantly interfere with the bioelectric circuitry of the human nervous system. As the energy resonance of the Earth alters over time this will undoubtedly affect how human DNA calibrates itself whenever a newborn enters the world.

An article in the journal *Bioelectromagnetics* entitled 'Do Electromagnetic Fields Interact Directly with DNA?' has stated that, 'Studies on DNA have shown that ... gene activation by magnetic fields could be due to direct interaction with moving electrons within DNA.'[12] The knowledge that the human nervous system can be influenced and modulated by frequencies (sound, light, language and thought) has been utilized by various spiritual traditions over the ages. This can be seen in the variety of exercises that use thought focus (prayer), sounds (music, chanting, singing), light (both natural light and produced light, such as in stained glass), and language (specific recitations such as *mantra* and *zikr*). Similarly, various shamanic practices have alluded to the notion that what we now understand to be DNA can be accessed through deliberate, conscious intention.[13] DNA appears to function, therefore, not only as a protein builder (the minority function) but also as a medium for the storage, receipt and communication of information. I would put forward that there is a new vibrational pattern descending upon our planet. Further, that the next stage in humanity's evolutionary development will involve a frequency shift in the vibrational patterns of our DNA. Of course, I cannot offer any concrete proof of this – call it inspired intuition!

If we understand that information is processed by us on a neurobiological level then we can accept that our nervous systems are channels for information. Furthermore, change within each individual will alter our biofields (DNA quantum fields) which through the process of resonance – entrainment[14] – will affect others around us. In this manner, a rising synchronization of human field frequency – and hence consciousness patterns – will come into effect. The psychic state of humanity can therefore be altered by what I referred to at the beginning of the chapter as the *DNA Frequency–Earth Alignment*. This entrainment process is what calibrates Earth energy and human DNA, and is part of our evolutionary 'work in progress'. Humanity is becoming conscious of itself in a way like never before. This is a physiological and psychological process – and one that may open our perceptions to the presence of multidimensional realities (*see* Chapter 11). Furthermore, since our DNA functions as a form of 'quantum antenna', it is possible that nonlocal information fields activate specific latent capacities within us when our state/frequency is ready for this. In this way, rather than considering that it is the human being who acts upon the DNA to 'activate' it (as some teachings indicate), it may well be the other way around. In other words, it is the DNA that, in response to particular influences, serves to activate specific dormant functions within the human being.

It is likely that our human DNA currently operates at a lower state of efficiency. I say this in part because our science can only point toward the visible 3% function of the DNA – in coding genetic instructions – whereas the 97% so-called 'junk DNA' still remains largely a mystery. I propose that the 97% 'unused' DNA is involved in interacting with other fields (quantum/electromagnetic) that are in harmony with the vibration of the planet. Still, I would venture that such functioning operates well below maximum potential. Since we know that DNA is present throughout our cellular structure we can be sure that our complete physiology is involved and related to our external energy fields and vibratory nuances. Since human DNA, and thus our cellular structure, is open to vibratory influence we must also address the possibility that our inner biology is open to the power of intent (thought forms/energy). According to many ancient teachings this is indeed the case,[15] and this has also been popularized in recent years by the plethora of self-help books which profess such things as success, health, riches, powers and the like, through the focused energies of intention. On a more profound level, however, it appears that part of our human DNA 'energy signature' can be recalibrated in our lifetime through exercising conscious compassion, awareness and various meditative practices. For many people, these are exactly the practices which have guided them through their lives, and indeed are part of the lives of many thousands of people. And this is a point worth considering: direct and/or indirect guidance (teachings, practices and so on) have always been required in preceding epochs as our terrestrial vibratory environment was not sufficient alone to provide the catalytic trigger. With the coming of the Phoenix Generation I feel this situation is changing.

The children born of the Phoenix Generation will organically, and in an unconscious way, exhibit increasing instances of direct informational exchange; that is, forms of inner knowing or gnosis. This gnosis is likely to be in the manner of informational exchange between the human nervous system and external 'intelligence' fields, which together feed information to the body–consciousness field. This shift will mark a transition to a self-initiated awakening in which individuals will be empowered without the need for groups or external teaching environments. Human spirituality is evolving, along with the realization that we are all quantum-entangled on a fundamental level. It may be the case that humanity has just been waiting for the establishment of an energetically conducive environment. And that time may now be at hand.

Fields of Resonance

For as long as humanity can perhaps remember this 'conducive environment' has been distorted through the presence and manufacture of fear and its associated vibrations of insecurity and anxiety. In terms of what we know about quantum coherence, it is likely that the vibrations of fear work to disable the overall quantum coherent field effect, thus disrupting contact with one's inner understanding. Fear serves to disempower the individual and cuts off the communication to the self. Yet the new children being born will play a great part in this shift away from the impacts of fear as they will instinctively not only move away from any vibrations (vibes) of fear but also, importantly, not be so affected by them. This is because on both a mental and emotional level they will no longer respond to old-paradigm attractors. The tentacles of fear and the need for giving away one's independence to external sources will not be a part of their paradigm. The shift is already under way in how the human being relates with a range of non-visible fields of information. As one writer has pointed out, 'The information you need is encoded in the structural makeup of every single cell in your body. Contact is there.'[16] This same source also noted that:

> When you are aware of your totality, the Life-impulse will transmit to you everything that you need to know in any given situation. Its message will always come as your first spontaneous impulse. Be attentive.[17]

The human capacity to achieve higher frequency-awareness is most likely a natural ability that we are each born with. Only, for most of us, this capacity has lain dormant as – like an under-exercised muscle – it was never properly used.

We now know through our latest scientific discoveries that the entire genetic information for a human body is contained in each of the body's many trillion cells. It could be the case – only speculative at this stage – that as humanity gradually increases its conscious awareness we will gain an inner intuitive access to the information that is enfolded in these communicating fields of energy. Our human physiology – DNA, cellular structure, nervous system, and so on – is likely to operate as a whole, coherent receiving apparatus that codes our fields of consciousness. Further, this bodily 'receiving apparatus' will seek to find resonance both above and below – that is, with Earth energies under our feet as well as electromagnetic fields above our heads, figuratively speaking.

Geologists are developing their understanding of how Earth energies are transmitted, along the surface of the crust as well as within the core of the Earth. Latest research indicates that the Earth's core behaves more along the lines of a crystalline structure rather than as the molten mass that many of us have as its image in our heads. In 1936 it was discovered (by the seismologist Inge Lehmann) that the Earth has a solid inner core distinct from its liquid outer core. This solid inner core was deduced by observing how earthquake-generated seismic waves were being reflected off the boundary of the inner core. Likewise, the outer core was found to be liquid, as earlier suspected. Yet what is interesting is that recent observations have shown that the inner core is not completely uniform. Rather, it contains large-scale structures indicated by seismic waves that pass more rapidly through some parts of the inner core than through others. It has even been suggested that the inner solid core is formed from iron crystals. What is known by science is that the inner core, through its dynamo action, plays a significant role in the generation of Earth's magnetic field.

Similarly, the crust of the Earth is known to support a network of energized, or 'magnetized' paths – variously called ley lines, Earth grid, pilgrimage routes and other names. In some form it appears that the Earth manifests particular tracks, or routes, of increased energy upon which it is said many ancient temples, ceremonial sites, gatherings and the like were built or held. Indeed, many gatherings and buildings today continue to be based upon certain accepted energized 'hot spots'.

Literally, then, the energy fields of the Earth pulsate under our very feet. In addition to this, above our heads the Earth's magnetic field, interacting with solar and cosmic rays, envelops humanity in a bubble of fluctuating energy. The human body is in relation – and thus some degree of resonance – with the gigantic energy generator that is our physical environment. Yet what about the non-physical environment?

Our latest science tells us that the Earth's electro-magnetic field is a sensitive membrane that responds to solar activity such as sun spot cycles, solar flares, coronal mass ejections and solar winds. We also know from neuroscience that human brain activity creates small electrical charges. Further, the human heart is now understood to act as a vibrant pump/generator of electromagnetic energy. Collate this with a human nervous system and cellular structure – thanks to DNA – that communicates as a coherent quantum field then we have intrinsic resonance between human biology and our terrestrial, solar and cosmic environments. Within this large collection of 'fields within fields' we have the phenomenon of consciousness which, it has been discovered, also functions as a field phenomenon. From this it is not such a large leap to connect with notions of a collective field of consciousness that has been referred to over the years as the *noosphere* (Teilhard de Chardin; Vladimir Vernadsky); *Overmind* (Sri Aurobindo); and the *world sensorium* (Oliver Reiser). We can also consider this 'overmind' consciousness as emerging as a form of planetary consciousness.

It is reasonable to consider, in this context, that par-ticular cosmic field effects impact DNA in living systems on this planet and serve as evolutionary triggers. Perhaps the last great 'cosmic wind' that blew acted to catalyze and accelerate the evolutionary development of *Homo sapiens* upon the Earth?

Whether we realize it consciously or not, our species is an agent of planetary change. We are deeply involved and have responsibility for assisting the transition to a planetary society. Humanity may also be instrumental in facilitating the emergence of a single planetary organism with a shared collective consciousness, a physical channel for the Overmind. This requires that humankind moves beyond the old mind of materialism and prepares for a psychic convergence worthy of a planetary species. We have arrived at the point where we need to interiorize the evolutionary process.

We may have to ask ourselves whether the planetary unification of conscious mind is an evolutionary imperative (perhaps it is the trajectory for all planets with biological life?). The psychic state of humanity appears to be undergoing an increased compression – or convergence – that may serve to synchronize life on this planet. This process, in fact, is nothing 'esoteric' as it has been part of human civilization from the first day our ancestors began to worship an external presence. The convergence of human consciousness/thought patterns takes place in ceremonial worship, and is central to human prayer. If we look at the *salat* practice of formal worship in Islam (it constituting one of the Five Pillars of Sunni Islam), we see that the worshipper is obliged to pray five times a day facing Mecca. These specifically designated times of concentrated states of mind create an intense convergence and focused stream of energy across the globe directed toward the geographical location of Mecca. We have many other forms of conscious convergence (or mental synchronization) upon this planet, throughout a myriad of social–cultural–religious–spiritual ceremonies, events or gatherings. The Global Consciousness Project,[18] established by Roger Nelson at Princeton University, for example, has demonstrated how human consciousness becomes coherent and synchronized at specific moments of worldwide impact (such as was noted on the day of Princess Diana's death). In the past, however, heightened synchronization in the human collective consciousness field was induced by external triggers. What I speculate is that our terrestrial–solar energy environment is undergoing a period of change that will assist in the internal activation of what we can loosely term transcendent states of consciousness. Specifically, our DNA Frequency–Earth Alignment resonance will increase in coherence and will result in humans organically possessing clearer access to living fields of information.

It is my sense that the Phoenix Generation will be among the first of those to awaken en masse to an era of instinctual gnosis. It will not necessarily mean that a person will be able to conduct a 'verbal conversation' with their inner cellular structure, as this is old-paradigm thinking. Yet it does signify that a growing generation of instinctively aware young children will inherently feel an *intentional* connection and communion with their whole being. And through this *intentional coherence* (or quantum resonance), a form of inner–outer balance will be felt. This 'felt sense' will be primary in guiding a young person in their life; providing trustful inner feelings and an instinctual sense of where one needs to go or what to do. As each person trusts this inner understanding, the energy of transformation will be dispersed throughout the already existing networks of connection and communication – exponentially empowering our planetary empathic mind. This, we can hope, will help to make our epochal and generational transition less turbulent and more organic. Rumi suggested this *intentional coherence* when he accurately wrote about the distinction between acquired and instinctive intelligence:

> *Two Kinds of Intelligence*
> There are two kinds of intelligence: One acquired,
> as a child in school memorizes facts and concepts
> from books and from what the teacher says,
> collecting information from the traditional
>   sciences
> as well as from the new sciences.
>
> With such intelligence you rise in the world.
> You get ranked ahead or behind others
> in regard to your competence in retaining
> information. You stroll with this intelligence
> in and out of fields of knowledge, getting always
>   more
> marks on your preserving tablets.
>
> There is another kind of tablet, one
> already completed and preserved inside you.
> A spring overflowing its springbox. A freshness

in the centre of the chest. This other intelligence
does not turn yellow or stagnate. It's fluid
and it doesn't move from outside to inside
through the conduits of plumbing-learning.

This second knowing is a fountainhead
from within you, moving out.[19]

This 'second knowing', which is the 'fountainhead'
within us, corresponds to a source of instinctual
knowing. Such an instinctual knowledge – rather than
acquired knowledge – is likely to be in harmony with
the integrated nature of our Earth systems. This, we can
expect, will be a factor in helping to transform many of
our planet's dysfunctional systems (*see* Chapter 10), as
well as re-aligning humanity into a balanced relationship
with our environment.

As more and more young people express their
awakening *instinctual intelligence*, more innovative
solutions to our global problems will emerge. It should
herald a catalytic effect, spearheading our civilization
into a quantum renaissance.

Chapter 10

A Quantum Renaissance

Biology and physics define the laws of a certain milieu or a
certain human fishbowl which endeavours to look at itself
or to look through the walls of its bowl, but when you
move to another milieu, as the amphibian one day emerged
into the open air of Life, the old laws fall away and another
unforeseeable 'life', or 'overlife', appears.

Satprem

We are not so much at the end of an era; rather we are
on the cusp of a new one emerging. Humanity is participating in the dynamic – and often chaotic – energetic
flux of evolutionary change. For all our technological
trappings and comforts we are little more than standing
on the adolescent shores of humanity's future. Our
current crises are not happenstance, but are the fires
that forge the catalysts – and bring the catharsis – of
change. Processes of evolution – social, cultural, self –
often use struggle as the impetus for creating real need.
And with the manifestation of such genuine necessity
often arises an organic, evolutionary response. Those
of us who constitute the Bridge Generation are already
feeling – and dealing with – these impacts and impetuses

for change and transformation. Just as evolution once thrust the fishes from the drying swamps, compelling them to discover another way to breathe under a new oppressive sun, so too are we compelled to forge from the ashes of our old ways a new vision of life:

> So we are landing in another air which will radically change the face of the Earth, which is pounding and kneading her unrelentingly to bring forth or forge a new species capable of bearing and living that Nectar she so much thirsts for.[1]

We are being compelled to forge within the crucible of our bodies – both the human and Earth bodies – a species that is not so much 'better' as it is *different*. We can look at the period of human history from our Stone Age ancestors to our present tribal–national–imperial stirrings as showing a species in gestation. We have been occupied with our outward gestures – our sabre-rattling – whilst on an almost invisible, yet parallel, path of inward evolutionary growth. The gestation period of humanity has lasted until a time when external conditions could match internal potentials. Such a possibility would set the stage for the emergence of a Planetary Human. This is what lies ahead for us as a quantum renaissance unfolds.

A collective force is arising through humanity that knows – *instinctively feels* – that other ways are now needed for the transition to a new era within sustainable and harmonious limits. This has never happened before because this point was never reached before. And humanity never reached this point before simply because it was not ready. New ideas are always things we've never thought of before – until they arrive. And they will arrive, increasingly so as we move into a time when the newer energies are forming and manifesting the seeds of the quantum renaissance. And with this newer seed energy will also emerge solutions to some of our most pressing problems – especially around energy and resources. The solutions are already there: we are just waiting for the 'Aha' moment! You don't have to believe me; just wait and see. There are people now who are working hard on the problems, and many young minds of the Phoenix Generation are soon going to join the laboratory of human problem-solving. Connecting, collaborating, sharing ideas and thoughts – the planetary membrane of consciousness is an active crucible of change and vision.

At each moment of need the human mind accesses solutions to overcome the current pressing problems. Once there were predictions that the world would run out of wood to burn – then coal extraction was developed. Then came the discoveries of oil and the large-scale production of electricity. Once again we are standing on the collective precipice of need – this need will trigger access to new solutions within us. The coming quantum renaissance will be a period of recalibration as structural changes will be implemented to accommodate these new developments. That is why it is important now to acquire an evolutionary perspective, one in which we understand that there are specific moments when sudden and innovative breakthroughs occur (what evolutionary biologists refer to as 'punctuated equilibrium').[2] Just as in our human fossil record, so too in our patterns of human thought there are long periods of stasis followed by sudden leaps of progress and change. Often in those periods of stasis the seeds of developmental change are planted. The farmer knows that planted seeds do not sprout overnight. Philosophers, artists, writers, mystics and creative-change agents, amongst others, have all worked to plant the seeds of evolutionary potential. Then when the right temperature arrives (when the 'cosmic wind blows'), the crops will gain their moment of optimum nutrition and push rapidly through the top-soil to partake of the sun's rays – rapid growth will thus occur. This is what is happening now.

Our seeds have been planted – and continue to be planted – and the new sun is radiating upon the Earth.[3] These seeds of radical and necessary change are beginning to poke through our planetary topsoil, and will be the harvest for the generations to come. We need to start getting excited about this – rather than lingering too long in the despondent waiting rooms of old energy. The cotton (your*self*) needs to get closer to the flame – if you wish it to be set alight! The quantum renaissance will allow each person to be comfortable with new under-standings of society and self – and not be overwhelmed by what may appear to be 'incredible possibilities'. Why, after all, should we wish to remain credible when we can, and should, be aiming for the incredible? The quantum renaissance will celebrate the inevitable transition to an era in which new models and thinking prevail. The struggling permutations of the upcoming years – like a metamorphosis period – will allow a new renaissance to birth. It will also celebrate different patterns of conscious thought emerging through humanity that will act as a waking epidermis upon the world. Teilhard de Chardin once described this as

> . . . a new envelope – the thinking envelope, more vibrant and a better conductor in a sense than any metal; more mobile than any liquid; more expansive than any gas, and more sensitive than all organic matter . . . [but] which could only come about through a crisis.[4]

The Phoenix Generation is here to plant the seeds of integrity in our social systems. This planting of the new consciousness and thinking patterns over the next couple of decades will bring a rich harvest in later years. The quantum renaissance will be an early stage in the emergence of these ideas. The mind of humanity that will be part of this renaissance will not only receive new thought impulses from the environment (*see* Chapter 9), but will also be bringing them into material manifestation and sharing them planet-wide. This is why I refer to this time as a quantum renaissance, as it will operate along the lines of a field effect – as an integrated whole – and not as separate national egos. It may indeed begin to emerge while the vestiges of national socio-cultural egos are vying for survival – yet these will soon become redundant, and irrelevant, evolutionary traits.

In a previous book Ervin László and I referred to this as the Akashic Age.[5] This explains how the latest in human scientific discovery – in the quantum realm – is helping to transform not only how we view the world, but how the fundamentals of our reality are constructed. As we progress in this knowledge – and I hope wisdom – this will shape how *our world informs us*. Furthermore, whilst this knowledge will be emerging from external channels of discovery, it will be matched by an increasing instinctual intelligence – gnosis – being received by those of the new Phoenix Generation. With this understanding manifesting in tandem, we are likely to see an exponential pace of development and discovery upon this planet. The quantum aspects that characterize our new sciences will come to represent the inherent features of the emerging renaissance.

This is the fundamental knowledge that will come to direct how we, as a conscious species, interpret and participate in a meaningful sense of reality. It will also come to underpin how we further develop our technologies. The people who will be teenagers and young adults around 2030 will instinctively grasp the underlying unity and oneness of humankind. They will have been born into a world where global perspectives and planetary friendships and conversations are the norm. They will consider themselves as citizens of the world first and foremost; they will be national participants only secondarily. Those of the Phoenix Generation will react against the automatic transmission of cultural conditioning. They will resist being filled with antiquated old-model thinking, invalid ideas and antiquated notions. They will not accept being a receptacle for outworn dogmas but will be open as a crucible for transmuting new ideas and ways into reality. The young people will know what will and what won't work – they won't try to fit old models into a time of new energy: only the 'old-mind crazies' will try that one! The young hearts and minds of the Phoenix Generation will be here to recalibrate life on Earth.

Recalibrations for a New Renaissance

The underlying quantum reality of our oneness and inherent connectivity will form the bedrock of understanding that will motivate the young people of the world to recalibrate this planet toward integrity. Behind this wish for integrity and transparency will be a central aspiration for well-being, harmony and compassion amongst peoples of the world. The Phoenix Generation will wish to see a better Earth. The human nervous system, as a frequency antenna, will be spreading the contagion of the new vibratory consciousness. At the point where humanity favours unification rather than separation, a great wave of new discoveries and inventions will flood the Earth. The quantum renaissance – *circa* 2030 – is likely to see significant changes and developments in the following areas: human spirit and wisdom; health; education and learning; media and lifestyle; new economics; technology; politics; new energies; and cosmic awareness.

i) Human Spirit & Wisdom

As already discussed, there will be a significant shift to recognizing and expressing our inner authority. Thus, we can envisage a move away from external dependencies to inner recognition and acceptance. This will manifest alongside what I have referred to in previous chapters as instinctual intelligence. Whereas in present times we tend to act from acquired information (based on educational conditioning), those of the Phoenix Generation will trust an internal sense of what needs to be done. This form of gnosis will be more in keeping with the harmonious relations of systems – environmental, social, cultural or technical. In other words, the emphasis will be upon coherence and balance.

Also, as each young person learns to trust their inner instinct, they will increasingly see through the fog of cultural lies. Throughout the upcoming years we will become more aware of the collective lies of our cultures. Each day more and more people will awaken to see the falsity, deceptions and the dances behind the shadows that are projected across our daily screens. Not only is 'All the world's a stage | And all the men and women merely players',[6] but that the *world is played* will become evident. As this unfolds it will be increasingly difficult for those behind the scenes of world affairs (sometimes referred to as the 'puppet masters') to manipulate and exploit the masses.

Along with the collapse of physical lies – those of economics, politics, health and the like – will be the collapse of falsehoods connected with religious doctrine, human potential and other-than-human intelligences. Humanity will begin to move out of its limiting confines – the prisons we have chosen to live within – and many straitjacket beliefs will fall away. One of these will be the belief that we are nothing more than physical human beings and that there are no other realms/dimensions of being beyond the earthly experience.

This will lead to revised interpretations of ancient wisdom as we awaken to the potential for change that is within each person. In this way there will be a recalibration of understanding; and a re-alignment of spiritual systems for a more enlightened consciousness. A new understanding and tolerance will respect the spiritual core of a person, and personal development and self-evolution will become core values. People will increasingly seek for, and respect the role of, wisdom within human institutions.

It will be evident that many younger people are being born with a sense of purpose – a calling activated within them. Many of them will arrive already activated as change agents. These young people will have a more polished communication with their inner self; and instead of having to 'name' or to 'categorize' their state (as we often do) they will simply *be* it and *live* it. We may even be tempted to refer to these new hearts and minds as the 'Love Generation', as they will seek to bring harmony and coherence into their lives. Theirs will be the manifesto of Love: to be a part of the world, as the world is a part of them; to be in communion with all living things and be in coherence with the planetary web of life; and to be in communion with fellow humans as a coherent community within a planetary society.

With these minds, hearts and spirit, the young people

of the quantum renaissance will develop a fresh understanding of our human health and wellness.

ii) Health

One of the major shifts will be a drastic turn away from belief, confidence and trust in the health industry. The health industry is currently a global trade that has commoditized human well-being into the industrialization of illness. The rise of 'big pharma', as it has been termed, has created a pharmaceutical conglomerate of global players that wield immense political influence. Theirs is an agenda that seeks to support a 'sickness for profit model' at the expense of natural, organic knowledge and well-being practices. Whilst this may seem a subjective critique, recent investigations and publications have shown an array of unethical and distasteful practices.[7] The basic premise of the old-paradigm 'illness industry' is that profits come before patients. Profits also come before transparent and objective research trials and results, according to many researchers. What we can say for sure is that the pharmaceutical lobby (also known as the drug lobby) exhibits its own unhealthy influence over politics and media representation. The result of this has already seen a loss of trust in the pharmaceutical industry, especially in the area of vaccinations. After the controversy surrounding the origins, media reaction and health industry response to the swine flu (H1N1 flu virus) incident of 2009, many people questioned the integrity of big pharma. The same could be said for the controversy around the MMR vaccine and autism.

However, despite these ongoing unresolved issues the main focus is on the new generation's increased intuition regarding their own health. The young people of the Phoenix Generation will listen more to their bodies; they will be more careful over what they ingest (food and medicine); and they will instinctively feel what their bodies need. This will occur parallel to a loss of 'public face' and reputation of big pharma as the new energies reveal the dishonesty of the incumbent industrialization of illness.

The global corporate health industry will be one of the major 'old-mind' systems to suffer at the hands of (r)evolutionary change. At the same time there will be increased confidence in and support of what are now considered 'alternative' health practices. This will emerge as our sciences continue to validate the principles and properties of the energetic universe that embeds us. The concept of energy exchange in healing will become more commonplace, and increasingly sought after. This includes the use of human consciousness in nonlocal healing. Medical doctor Larry Dossey has publicized how scientific facts and evidence are confirming our nonlocal nature. Dossey states that this development will usher in what he calls Era III medicine, that is transpersonal or nonlocal medicine (Era 1 is mechanical medicine; and Era II is mind–body medicine). Era III medicine, according to Dossey, accounts for abilities/capacities of the non-local mind – telepathy, distance-healing and related phenomena. These attributes have often been referred to as 'distant intentionality'.[8] The renaissance will be a time

181

when illness is recognized not solely as an individual matter, but as something which affects others around us. As Dossey says, our 'bondedness is fundamental, natural, factory installed, the way things are'.[9]

Era III medicine, in recognizing nonlocal healing, will become central to how health is viewed and understood in the post-big-pharma years. Era III medicine recognizes that consciousness is fundamental and therefore forms a perspective of healing that recognizes the funda- mental, infinite nature of our field-connectedness. In the beginning the older doctors will have a hard time accepting this transition. However, as those of the Phoenix Generation assume doctors' roles themselves they will usher in this new period for human health. Health and illness will be viewed as transitional states – even death will be recognized as a transitional moment – and thus empathy, compassion and love will play greater roles in the process of healing. Already we have the early signs of Era III medicine and health practices emerging among open-minded doctors and patients around the world, and in many other incidents rarely publicized.

Human connections are transpersonal and nonlocal, as evidenced by the healing work of Adam McLeod. Adam, a renowned international healer and speaker, has been healing people since he was a young boy. According to Adam, every physical object emits information in the form of quantum data – as a quantum hologram or image – regardless of where it is located. The body's field of quantum information is then accessed and assessed by the healer. Of this Adam says,

Our consciousness and the universal consciousness is an interconnection of constant information exchange. Some day, a truth as obvious as this won't have to be seen as self-revelation but instead will be readily accepted.[10]

When we are conceived, says Adam, biophoton emissions start co-ordinating the development of our cells so that the goal of every cell is to communicate in harmony with every other cell. This is because as soon as light begins co-ordinating the formation of our cells, consciousness emerges. Our brains act to access the quantum energy fields around us to organize, process and interpret this information so that it has local meaning for us. In this way direct nonlocal information is brought into a local, cognitive and meaningful reality for us. Adam suggests that we can each exercise our connection to the nonlocal quantum field just like exercising a muscle; he advises that we practise paying more attention to our intuition, or gut instinct. Everything in this context is a complex array of vibrating frequencies, with certain frequencies having specific information. Consciousness does not reside solely in the brain, but is within every atom, cell and subatomic particle that constitutes the human body. This parallels exactly what some of the latest discoveries in the new sciences are finding out. Adam believes that the flow of energy/information, and our access to it, are constantly evolving and changing. With continued evolution, he notes, we will be able to access information from the field more easily.[11]

This is precisely what will be emerging during the

quantum renaissance: greater access to the quantum field through an increased instinctual intelligence. We will not necessarily be thinking 'Okay, I'm accessing the quantum information field now!' – yet in a natural way people will be able to receive information from their biofield about the health of their body. That is why trust in orthodox, corporate medicine will have been eroded and replaced by more energy-based healing and other practices now considered 'alternative' or 'fringe'. The years of this emerging renaissance, *circa* 2030, will usher in more education and new understanding about health, biology and the nature of illness and disease. Because of this new wave of information and understanding, our human selves – as well as our human sciences – will help humans to live longer.

Extended life will go hand in hand with surprising research findings about the nature of human DNA. We will come to realize that DNA acts to activate specific energies within us when our state/frequency is ready for this. In other words that human DNA activates specific dormant functions within the human being according to evolutionary necessity. DNA will finally be accepted as an unfolding process, rather than as a static 3% protein-building set of chemical reactions. This unfolding process occurs in a quantum, nonlinear way, and will be grasped in an intuitive way, helping people to have more natural insight into their well-being.

As a consequence our health diagnoses will have less dependency on clinical observations and more trust in instinct. Increased intuition about our own health will guide us in choosing what changes we need to instigate. It will become more common for people to express the feeling, and intention, that they are in communication with their cells (or their 'cellular self').

The development of personal well-being and health, with extended lives, will lead not to an increasing population but rather to a decrease. This will be because there will be a decline in the need for larger 'survival families', as is often the case in current developing nations. The instinct will shift more toward smaller families that can provide close care and nurture. Couples of the Phoenix Generation who live in high-population regions may even opt out of raising children. States are likely to begin experiencing a decline in population around 2030 rather than an increase. Human thinking will simply choose to do things differently – old patterns will shift. Finally, our planetary society will stabilize its population growth in line with sustainable limits. Living within sustainable limits will form part of the understanding shared within the redesigned educational platforms.

iii) Education & Learning

The antiquated educational systems will find themselves going through a radical rethinking and revision as a response to students' needs and attitudes. Classrooms will no longer be contained within four-walled rooms: learning spaces will be more interactive, incorporating many features of online contact and group participation. Some of these will include working online alongside students from around the world; learning from virtual game-puzzles and online multimedia presentations; and connecting with learning environments that make use of various platforms.

The student learning environment will become an open collaborative space (with MOOC – massive open online courses) that connects to other learning spaces across the planet – both physical and virtual. This will expand the range of peer-teaching and peer-learning. Not only will students have access to a varied range of teachers but they will also learn from peers around the world. Teaching will not be limited to the 'one person at the head of the class' model; older people, retired persons, volunteers around the world and others will make themselves available in specially designated online platforms to offer their services for questions and learning forums. Guests from varied occupations – business leaders, scientists, creative artists, consultants, and so on – will regularly join online learning forums to interact gladly with students and to pass on their own learning and knowledge.

Online '3-D world' platforms will also be developed as immersive learning experiences. Some teaching institutes will create fully working virtual campuses (an extension from the online campus) in which students can enrol as avatars and attend virtual classes populated by students from around the world. The learning process will shift from being a linear two-way model (teacher–student) to a multi-phase process incorporating a variety of learning possibilities with mixed-level collaborators. These mixed learning environments – no longer called classrooms – will also place students of varying ages and abilities together. In this way older, more learned students, can also assist in the learning process of lower-level students.

Learning environments will no longer depend upon location since many learning–teaching platforms will use an array of online and virtual collaborative spaces. Furthermore, the learning process will be made more fun. It will allow for a broad range of creativity and 'free time' for brainstorming (heart-storming) ideas. The interaction between students and their varied teachers will be mutual and not one-way. Students will have more influence in directing their learning process according to their needs, wishes and motivations. The old-model curriculum of preparing students for an industrial workforce will no longer apply. The world will have changed in a way that will have made many older needs obsolete. The students of the Phoenix Generation will also have a greater instinctual understanding of what they feel is necessary to learn for each individual. The 'one-model-fits-all' rule will no longer apply and will have been phased out. Learning modules will become more individually customized. Importantly, the 'stick–carrot' reward system will also go the way of the dinosaurs. The older examination system will be replaced by a variety of comprehension/capacity feedback from both teachers and peers. Understanding will be measured by one's comprehension and individualized capability – not by standardized grades. Stress and self-doubt will be replaced by enjoyment and self-confidence.

The educational system will celebrate knowledge rather than box it. There will still be businesses that will attempt to establish a form of 'cognitive capitalism' (with knowledge as a paid-for commodity) – yet this model will be rejected by the new young minds. Traditional 'knowledge' subjects – mathematics, science, history and others – will still be offered; however, they will be accompanied by a variety of modules more suited to the practical and creative needs of the era. It will seem as if there is an endless array of topics for the student to connect with. Such new learning environments will thus influence young people into how they relate to mainstream media.

iv) Media & Lifestyle

The new minds will have had enough of a fear-mongering, fear-sponsoring media. They will reject the endless drivel that is splashed across our mainstream broadcast channels. This may sound optimistic in an age in which consumption and consumerism have reached a peak. Yet it was the energies of the old era that pacified and nullified the minds of youngsters. The 'distraction of the self' belonged to an age when lies masqueraded as truths; and the naked emperor was praised as wearing an Armani suit. As instinctual intelligence becomes more manifest, the false façades will drop and it will be more difficult to sideline people into controlled distraction through entertainment trivia. The old programming that dominated the mainstream media in past decades offered only a crude and brutal vision that delighted in high-tension and stressful drama, in conflicts, murder and sexual espionage. Such programming did not inspire nor elevate people toward higher ideals. There was little balance or harmony in such a flickering kaleidoscope of images. Yet this will change.

There will be a shift in media programming toward what elevates a person rather than what closes them down. This shift will be brought about by an increasing demand for more informative programming. The young minds and hearts of the Phoenix Generation will increasingly reject negative news and influences, and naturally shift away from such energies. The mainstream media will be forced – through viewing figures and thus advertising revenue – to broadcast more inspiring and uplifting programmes. Also, the mainstream media will be impacted greatly by the rapid rise of community media. The larger corporations will continue to merge as they will find it difficult to exist in a people-centred environment that increasingly rejects their style of broadcast. Peer-to-peer programming, from the people, will become more popular as people prefer to produce and share their own news, stories and events. What is now termed the 'alternative media' will be more significant as people share between their networks the stories that inspire and interest them. So not only will community media see a revival – thanks in large part to appropriate technology – but also self-produced media will become more the norm. Those of the Phoenix Generation will themselves be content-producers – producing, creating and distributing their own inspired content-driven media. The top-down corporate-controlled media will no longer be the dominant force. This will also reflect changes in lifestyle.

People will seek out those experiences and impacts that are positive, and that bring harmony to life rather than disorder. Desirable traits sought within the modern renaissance lifestyle will include peacefulness, harmony, coherence, non-judgement, forgiveness, conscious communication, love, understanding, transparency, honesty, integrity, and of course humour. There will be a greater general appreciation of the role and place of meditation within peoples' lives. During the years leading up to the quantum renaissance more and more people will be shifting their priorities in life, seeking out meaning and well-being in place of career status and money. This will manifest over the years in many people leaving their traditional employment and looking for alternative ways to support themselves that are more conducive to inner development and well-being. This will also result in many people leaving their current homes, especially if they are within crowded urban areas or joyless suburban neighbourhoods, and searching for more nourishing environments to live in. This is likely to result in a revitalization of communities in more rural locations, with an emphasis upon sustainability.

The creative minds of the Phoenix Generation will strive to construct new ways of doing things that are more harmonious with environmental and ecological systems. New sustainable lifestyles will emerge rapidly as people seek well-being and personal meaning that are in coherence with physical limits and resources. New communities, towns, villages and regions will adjust to do things differently in alignment with the new frequencies, in harmony with the growing inner authority of the younger generations. There will be an unprecedented emergence of innovative systems to tackle current issues and future needs in such areas as economics, technology and energy.

v) New Economics

Innovative models that we have not yet conceived of will come into being and provide creative solutions to local and global needs. As discussed in Chapter 7, distributed assistance in the way our systems work will manifest new paradigms – and new business plans – that are based on a future that is decentralized and co-operative. In the quantum renaissance we will learn to live beyond our imagination. A newly formulated international financial-credit system will be created that is transparent rather than opaque, and not run by private individuals/organizations. The corrupt international economic system of the early 21st century will be no more. It is abundantly clear that the perpetual growth paradigm of 20th-century economics is not a viable option for maintaining a coherent and stable economic framework.

Those of the Phoenix Generation will grow up in a world where governments are learning the lesson that a new economics must take into account not perpetual growth but perpetual happiness and well-being. Following the footsteps of Bhutan's Gross National Happiness index, different regions will consider their wealth based on the well-being of their peoples. Gross National Happiness will be more important than Gross National Product in a world in which new minds are looking to create a sustainable, long-term future for the planet.

By 2030 we will see a mixture of localized and global economic systems operating together. The localized models will be based on local physical currencies that support regional businesses and projects. The global systems are likely to be based upon fewer currencies (or credits) that are agreed upon by the international community – rather than being pegged to a particular currency favouring one nation. The new economics will be more tangibly connected to value and worth, rather than to virtual hoarding and unsustainable speculating. Regional and international economics will value people and their unique contributions, as the true wealth of a region will be measured by the well-being and happiness of the people within. Debt will no longer be the principal economic driver. This will release people from debt bondage and other forms of forced social indenture. A new economics will be seen as a force for creativity, innovation and development, rather than as a process that burdens and restricts people. A new economics will be seen as an energy of circulation; this will include a new array of innovative funding options that will emerge to help small, local projects meet local needs across the globe.

The new renaissance economics will be based on the

quantum nonlocal model in which everything connects. People across the world will contribute in funding the projects they relate to and agree with. In a system that develops from the previous crowd-funding model, people everywhere will act as the shareholders, receiving a share in profits. Global economics will no longer need to rely on top-down funding, as it develops a strong and reliable decentralized model. This will not neglect the role of larger corporations; younger innovative minds will increasingly take on major roles in businesses of the future. Many corporations and businesses will have to undergo considerable restructuring in order to survive the transition into the new era. This restructuring will ensure that they are more responsive to peoples' needs, as well as the need to invest in the new thinking for a viable future.

The new economics will shrug off the old image of economics as being a source of manipulation and instead will rise as an energy for manifesting and implementing solid and positive change in the world. It will embrace the decentralized, connected culture and begin to operate more freely between people in a way that is not restricted solely to financial exchange. An economics of welfare and well-being based on the exchange of services and assistance will also be prominent among the new generations: altruism will replace austerity.

The rise in well-being and networks of economic altruism will also be supported and promoted by emerging new technologies.

vi) Emerging Technologies

The exponential rate of discovery in the coming decades of the 21st century will be extraordinary. Those of the Phoenix Generation will be born into a world in which new technologies of communication and collaboration will enhance the connection with the world around them. The fears over privacy, data-collection, and of a surveillance society were attached to the 'old-mind' model use of technology that played a role in developing globalization and authoritarian governance. These fears may be dominant in the early stages until the new thinking is able to align technologies with models of transparency and open co-operation. Technologies will then be developed that will lay the framework for a planetary society based on ethics of sharing and openness alongside respect for privacy. Technologies of communication and connection will continue to foster a sense of togetherness amongst people worldwide.

The burgeoning 'cloud space' will further add to the sense of moving through a 'seamless' environment in which technologies will increasingly be embedded in our everyday world. This will further nurture the sense of living in a quantum era when instant connectivity and sharing will become second nature to the younger minds. It will become increasingly evident that human technologies *external* to us are only manifesting a reality that already exists *within* us. Simultaneous instant communication across space and time will nurture within the Phoenix Generation a sense of living within a planetary society. They will feel in constant contact with like-minded people across the world. This connectivity will help to stimulate and catalyze species empathy as people will feel an innate sense of being internally and energetically connected to others. The instinctual intelligence within the younger generations especially will be shared around the world instantly. This fostering of collaboration will lead to an acceleration in inventions and new discoveries.

Quantum computing will be a main driver in the development of a new generation of technologies. This will emerge alongside the new sciences providing quantifiable evidence, as well as applied understanding, of quantum energy (that is, the scientific ability to see and measure quantum energy). This will pave the way for a rewrite of human scientific knowledge. Quantum computing and quantum science will work to form the foundations of an era that at its heart will radically change the way human beings communicate and interact with their surroundings and the living universe. It is likely that during this time a form of *quantum communication* will be developed that will allow humanity to attempt contact with other intelligences in the galaxy. This physical technology will exist alongside our 'internal technologies' that will also be opening up to greater forms of contact (including telepathic ones). It will be evident during the renaissance years that humanity is not alone within the cosmos. The next evolution of quantum technologies will be the breakthrough we have been waiting for in our bid to make verifiable contact with other intelligences in the universe.

The Phoenix Generation will also be pioneers in a new generation of biotechnology. The 'old mind' thinking of biotechnology is focused on modifying the function and behaviour of microbes and living organisms to improve performance. This may range from enhancing the human body – recombinant gene technologies and immunology therapies – to bioengineering. The future of technologies is not so much in their upgrading capacities but in their convergence. The whole plethora of emerging technologies – nano/bio-technology; synthetic and quantum biology, quantum computing and others – is increasingly set to merge so that the very definition of life will be questioned. The renaissance will be the beginning of bringing technology 'alive'. As DNA is increasingly combined into both computing and synthetic biology we will witness the early stages of a new biotech creation phase that will mark this era as the birth age of *living technology*. After this time the chief feature of modern technologies of human civilization will be the fact that they will be a part of the Earth's living ecosystem. This (r)evolutionary renaissance will catalyze the next era that will be known as 'The Age of Planetary Awakening'.

vii) Politics

Democracy has thus far been known to be corrupt, misleading and inefficient. It has been democracy in name only, despite the relatively progressive nature of Western politics. It has still not truly been a political process representative of the people – especially when the choices for voting are so limited. It has been similar to deciding between two varieties of product on the shop shelf (only to find out later that both products are owned by the same multinational company). The truth is that despite calling itself 'democracy' it was never a truly inclusive and transparent political process. In the upcoming years technologies for more inclusive and participatory democracy will emerge that will benefit the people. So-called 'political parties' will not be exclusively for politicians. The domain of politics will diversify and will include people from all areas of life to represent local, national and international regions. Governments and the political process will not exclusively be the domain of career politicians: they will be comprised of representatives from all walks of life. These will include, but not be limited to, civil society, community representatives, trade representatives, scientists, well-known thinkers/intellectuals, architects/designers, and cultural creatives and artists. Furthermore, each person (voter) will be able to participate in the various stages of the political process through digital forms of involvement.

The new young voters of the Phoenix Generation will not want the old energy from the previous era. The youthful energies of change will no longer accept the bickering and name-calling that has generally been called 'politics'. The new minds will wish for integrity, honesty and transparency in the political process, irrespective of geography and culture. There will no longer be any space for the old debates – politics will have to drop the crude, often simplified and manufactured discussions of Left vs. Right; Capitalism vs. Anti-capitalism; Democratic vs. Republican, and the rest. The old-energy mentality will wish to continue fighting over these ruptured and antiquated distinctions; yet the energy of the new mind will no longer accept their rudimentary and divisive tactics. Increasing human awareness and instinctual intelligence will see through the two-dimensional theatrical charade that was once used to sway the masses. Those of the Phoenix Generation will instinctively know that the most destructive decision that an individual can make is to give away their own authority and decision-making power. This new era of change will herald the rise of participatory politics.

There will still be leaders in the field of politics, as there will be in other fields, yet there will emerge a wave of conscious leaders who will not be out to sell themselves on superficial short-term promises. The new leaders who will emerge from among the Phoenix Generation will be fully involved in participatory politics, and will know that they are in position to listen to the feedback of others. The new wave of leaders will instinctively understand that theirs is a planetary society where a long-term future vision is required. This long-term political perspective will instinctively embrace a planetary perspective in which peoples, nations, issues and needs are all woven together into a penetrating and interlacing tapestry. Participatory politics inherently recognizes that any regional problems and issues are global ones too and therefore shared. The young leaders of the Phoenix Generation will carry the new energy into the conflict regions, such as the Middle East and Africa. The new wave to emerge in politics will not be confined to the so-called 'industrialized' nations but will, importantly, rise up and develop in those areas most in need. The political processes that will survive the transition years of the next two decades will be those that represent the participatory spirit of the people. The survival of politics as we know it will depend on the ability of people and processes to recalibrate to receive, and be in alignment with, the intensifying energy of awakening human consciousness. Our digital technologies will ensure that participatory politics is a practical reality. The generations to come will ensure that the practical reality becomes a genuine one.

The goal of participatory politics that is set to emerge around 2030 will have peace as a priority and political responsibility. The peace of unity upon a diverse planet will be one of the radical emerging energies to signify a change in direction for our planetary species. It will not happen overnight and will need time and effort. Nor will it be the only radical energy rising up with the Phoenix Generation.

viii) New Energies

The increased necessity to find new energy resources will be a central issue for those of the Phoenix Generation. For them it will be a priority to develop solutions to many related problematic global issues such as pollution, monopolies, scarcity, unsustainability, energy costs and others. Due to this critical necessity, these young and inspiring minds will not accept the obstacles from the older industrial world. Not only will the younger generations forge forward with dedication and enthusiasm, they will also be more strongly connected to an instinctual intelligence that influences a particular manner of perception.

A new energy source – or sources – will be discovered for the next phase of our transition toward a planetary society. It is likely that the components for this energy shift have been with us for some time. However, it will take the convergence of forces – new sciences, new consciousness, and new necessities – for it to manifest. The new energy source will neither be centralized nor monopolized. It will be focused on the local production/procurement and distribution of a type of renewable energy. It is more likely to be procured than produced since it will be sourced from an ever-present energy potential. At its heart may be access to what is termed quantum energy (also referred to as zero-point energy or vacuum energy). Other forms of energy likely to be further developed are magnetism/electromagnetism and cold fusion. The renaissance will provide a renewed spurt of motivation to discover innovative new processes of energy that will abolish the energy monopolies from the Industrial Revolution.

It may be difficult for some people to visualize or conceive of the next energy revolution, as it has not yet arrived. What can be said is that it will be as radically different as oil was from wood. When a 'new source' is discovered – and it will be – it will revolutionize the entire fabric of our planetary civilization. This is not fanciful rhetoric – we only have to look at how the world was changed through the exploitation of oil to see a precedent. The way of life of many societies during the past 150 years has been heavily dependent upon the lubricant of oil: our industries (plastics, machinery, cosmetics, construction, medicine, domestic appliances); our food systems (fertilizers, packaging, conservation, distribution); our transport (cars, aircraft and the rest); our wars (of course!); and so on. Human civilization has in the previous century designed, constructed and developed a global society based upon the presence of oil as the primary energy resource. That is why this 'oil era' has to change as part of the transition – it is unsustainable and can no longer grow or evolve. The next phase of our evolution as a planetary civilization will be marked by the discovery – and thus arrival – of an alternative source of energy that will literally power our planetary society into being and radically alter its very landscape.

It is unlikely that the next source of our power will be based on the alternative power sources we have currently been utilizing, such as basic solar power, tidal and wind power and others. Whilst these are functional as localized power sources they are not sufficient to supply the entire, and varied, needs for a planetary civilization to grow. The sun, for example, is a power source, yet its energy cannot be adequately distributed in a concentrated form suitable and sufficient for planetary needs. There will, however, be a variety of smaller energy 'innovations' made possible by new technologies, such as providing fresh water for the planet by inexpensive and simple methods of desalination. A likely contender for this will be the use of magnetism for the desalination mechanism – a relatively simple yet still non-utilized process. Yet as part of the grand transition it is likely that a new 'quantum based' source will be discovered, and preparations will be under way to make this accessible for humanity.

The important point will be that this new source of power will be available everywhere as it will exist all around us. With this the case, we will see the collapse of the major oil/energy conglomerates as they will be forced to shift their focus and strategies. These energy corporations may fragment into serving niche and/or industrial markets through energy/oil subsidiaries, yet most mass needs will be provided for by the radical breakthrough of a new 'planetary energy' source. The arrival of this new energy source will revolutionize social organization on planet Earth and consolidate the path toward a planetary society.

The new decentralized energy networks that will emerge as a response will influence the growth of self-sufficient communities within larger regional areas – smaller systems within larger systems – that will lead to the increased celebration of locality and place within a more connected and established global society. Decentralized networks of energy distribution will also affect living and working patterns, as decentralization opens up possibilities of living comfortably in less dense and urbanized areas. It is likely that major cities will start to decrease in size (especially in the West) as more and more people move away as small-community life becomes once again more favourable. People will be able to work and communicate with the world from any location, thus altering social and work patterns. Cities are likely to remain as production/work zones as new innovative inventions and technologies allow this gradual shift. The arrival of a new planetary energy source will piggy-back on existing decentralized networks that were initially developed as a 'stepping-stone' away from the centralized grid structure. By the time the quantum renaissance emerges many decentralized energy networks will already exist – as if waiting!

Many new developments will emerge that are more likely to find research funding from both creative apolitical sources (individuals worldwide) as well as from non-governmental sources eager to assist humanity. The energy revolution that will emerge over these years will catalyze new thinking, designs, architecture, transport, social life, work, global finance, interstellar travel, and many more activities, in ways we are unable to conceptualize now. It will truly be a (r)evolutionary catalyst that will open up not only our planet but also our human awareness and consciousness to the presence of a dynamic, energetic and living universe. The next energy phase will be humanity's breakthrough on the way to true human–cosmic awareness.

ix) Cosmic Awareness

A recalibration of human awareness is already happening, yet this will become even more apparent as we move nearer to 2030 and the emerging renaissance. A gradual shift in human awareness will also emphasise human integration and integrity, which will affect the systems we have in place in the world (as discussed above). Yet we are talking here about a generational change that will manifest over years – and decades – and will unfold in a way that will help to normalize the transition. There is nothing that will occur to create an 'esoteric New Age' era upon the Earth. The whole point of this unfolding evolutionary process is that it has to happen naturally, organically, and it has to adjust and calibrate within a functioning human social environment. True harmony is about coherence and fitting in – it is not about going all weird or 'way out' just to prove something is different. The 'new difference' is that new patterns of awareness and conscious thinking will co-create a way of living and being that will replace our older models and ways. It will be a wonderfully cohesive and organic process. In fact, it is only human stubbornness that may make it a prickly and sometimes uncomfortable experience!

The patterns of human awareness set to emerge will show understanding and acceptance of the variety of cultural differences that make up our beautiful planetary species. The awareness of those of the Phoenix Generation will show heightened levels of tolerance and sensitivity. Also, significantly, as individual gnosis develops so will an instinctual understanding of a human–cosmic connection – what can be referred to as cosmic humanism. This cosmic humanism emerging within a new young generation of humanity will include the understanding that not only is a specific planetary organism being formed, but also that humanity is developing an organ of cosmic communication and connectivity.

Each human is birthed into the world with an internal 'knowing' or 'sense' – even a yearning – for a connection that binds the human to a greater truth. In recent human history this innate inner sense has been translated into external institutions and structures called religion (from the Latin verb *religare* – to bind). The bond of the human with a greater cosmic intelligence has been, over time, re-directed into obedience to orthodox human edifices and rituals. In this we have lost our own internal authority and connection. Now this inner bond and connectivity is returning to humanity, and will manifest more strongly in the gnosis of those of the Phoenix Generation. When this is coupled with the new scientific understanding that forms the foundation of the quantum renaissance, humanity will once again gain awareness of its inherent cosmic connectedness. Not only will it become acceptable to regard the cosmos as a dynamic, living intelligence, but humanity will also recognize the reality of galactic civilizations.

Life upon planet Earth will come to see itself as a family among families; humanity will be seen as an intrinsic part of our fellow planetary, solar, cosmic and universal families. Humanity's conditioning veil will be lifted and an internal realization will transform our organs of perception. Humanity will come to see itself as having not only a place within the larger cosmic picture but also a role and a responsibility. Those of the Phoenix Generation will bring forth new perspectives on the universe that will be the beginning of humanity's multi-dimensional journey.

Chapter 11

Normalizing the Multiverse

Now the Permanent staff on Earth have always had one main task, which is to keep alive, in any way possible, the knowledge that humanity, with its fellow creatures, the animals and plants, make up a whole, are a unity, have a function in the whole system as an organ or organism . . . as part of Nature, plants, animals, birds, insects, reptiles, all these together making a small chord in the Cosmic Harmony.

Doris Lessing, Briefing for a Descent into Hell

Perception rides upon the expressions of the heart like a canoe rides upon the waters.

Ken Carey, Return of the Bird Tribes

Human awareness is the real game-changer. Human awareness alters our perceptions and transforms the vision we have of the world. Our awareness and perception of our place in the world and in the 'bigger picture' are ultimately a question of consciousness. When human consciousness changes – *everything* changes. Evolution, in this perspective, is all about degrees of consciousness. Consciousness is that which connects – it is an energy that binds us all. When one person 'wakes up' – becomes more consciously aware – this helps others to awaken also. By being aware, we help others to be aware also. This is the exponential beauty of the 'energy-that-binds': consciousness. As I discussed in previous chapters, there is a shifting level of consciousness–awareness unfolding upon this planet, which is due in part to a resonance between human physiology and Earth's vibrational energy signature. The coherence between information fields – biological–environmental–quantum – is increasing, thus manifesting in new generations of humans that show increased instinctual intelligence and a greater cosmic humanism.

We can visualize this as the new consciousness operating as sound/vibration waves that will recalibrate our older models and patterns and provide for us a new 'blueprint'. Consider how sound/vibration waves can alter matter: particles scattered on a surface are reformed into new orderly geometric shapes in response to changing sound vibrations.[1] A new 'sound vibration' – or energy signature – entering our collective energy field will recalibrate human consciousness into a new mode. By altering the 'pattern recognition' of the conscious field of humanity we may gradually begin to perceive the real existence of other-dimensional perspectives. In other words, humanity is on a path to recalibrate its potential to receive, and transcribe, other types of energy and form. By altering its capacity to receive other wavelengths of information, humanity will be broadening its awareness, understanding and connection with a greater range of dimensional realities. We may then come to realize that we exist in a particular universe that reflects our energy state; intelligent life exists in a wondrous profusion of multiverses. We will surely then need to change our antiquated responses to the question 'What is life?'

The 'official mythology' that has dominated recent scientific consensus and human thought is that we were lucky enough to find ourselves in a 'just-right' universe – a universe that happens to have been created by chance. And now we are struggling for survival on a dead chunk of rock hurtling through 'empty' space in a so-far lifeless universe. Sounds a bit like a prison to me! However, according to the calculations of mathematical physicist Roger Penrose, the probability of randomly coming across such a universe as we find ourselves in – fine-tuned to life – is 1 in $10^{10^{123}}$.[2] With these incredible odds there would, somewhat ironically for science, be more 'chance' of living in an intelligent universe! It would seem more reasonable to conclude that it is misguided human thinking that cannot accept that the universe is biased toward life. Let us not forget that life has been returning again and again on planet Earth after each major extinction event.[3] Is it reasonable to assume that such persistence does not occur in a random universe not biased toward life? However, the mythology of living in a dead universe has been compatible – dare we say 'useful' – with the consumerist lifestyle that has been a dominant ideology for much of modern life. If we are living a life of blind chance within a world of lifeless, materialistic forces then does it not seem reasonable that humanity should exploit its surroundings to make the best it can for itself? In this scenario, human life – our existence – has no greater purpose or meaning.

Yet, as I have endeavoured to show throughout this book, our worldviews are changing in line with the recalibration of human consciousness. What may have seemed reasonable to us yesterday – or even today – will appear antiquated and simplistic to those generations to come. As Nobel laureate Doris Lessing wrote:

> What we live through, in any age, is the effect on us of mass emotions and of social conditions from which it is almost impossible to detach ourselves. Often the mass emotions are those which seem the noblest, best and most beautiful. And yet, inside a year, five years, a decade, five decades, people will be asking, 'How could they have believed that?'[4]

Indeed, the young hearts and minds of the Phoenix Generation will wonder how humanity could have believed in a purposeless dead universe for so long. They will instinctively feel within themselves the reality of vibrant and dynamic multiverses all teeming with life – and they will be reaching out with intent to connect with this reality. In this way how our species, as part of a planetary society, perceives the significance of life will greatly shift. For the first time in our known history, humanity will begin collectively to engage with, and participate consciously in, its evolutionary purpose.

The early footprints of these steps are already there in the sand, waiting for many others to follow in the same or similar tracks. Nobel Prize-winning scientist Francis Crick, co-discoverer of the DNA sequence, could not understand how even a single assembled protein could have emerged by chance. Crick calculated the odds of this happening as just 1 chance in 10^{260}: this is an incredible (and immeasurable) sum when we consider that all the atoms in the entire observable universe have been calculated to amount to 'only' 10^{80}. Both Crick and astronomer Fred Hoyle believed that life was already too complex when it first appeared on Earth and thus must have originated from elsewhere, off-planet. Hoyle is now infamous for stating, somewhat controversially, that for complex life to have originated by chance is statistically as likely as a hurricane blowing through a scrap yard and producing a Boeing 747. Hoyle also supported the general panspermia hypothesis[5] which states that life exists throughout the universe and is distributed by bacteria being present on passing/crashing meteoroids, asteroids and planetoids. Similarly, Crick famously stated that since it was highly unlikely that complex forms of bacteria on Earth arose by random chance it was therefore more likely that they arrived on Earth by what is known as 'Directed Panspermia'.[6] This proposes that the seeds of life (perhaps early bacterial forms of DNA) may have been purposely spread by advanced extraterrestrial civilization(s). The reasons for this could be many, such as an advanced civilization facing extinction; as a means for terraforming planets, perhaps for later colonization; or as a design to spread the spiritual seeds of life within a particular universe/ dimension. Crick concludes his hypothesis by stating that DNA is 'not of this Earth'.

Our consensus paradigms of 'what is life' are being rocked by the latest findings from science. Inexplicable to the current state of knowledge is the recent finding that organic molecules are produced in stars.[7] What this means is that the basic substances on which life are based (as we know it) are already produced in the evolution of stars. Organic molecules necessary for life are created in the deep furnaces of stellar evolution and then ejected into surrounding space. These molecules may then coat clumps of interstellar matter that then subsequently condense into other stars and planets. This understanding could offer us another picture of how organic matter arises in the universe. This picture shows us a universe that is a veritable factory for life, with stars pumping and spewing out the molecules for creation like huge generators all dotted across the universe. The lifeless rock idea just got . . . well, even more lifeless!

Once we accept that we exist within an immense universe teeming with the potential for life, it is a natural next step to question whether other conscious intelligences exist 'out there'. A follow-on question might be whether transpersonal states of consciousness can form a connection with other intelligences and/or dimensional realms? In fact, this very question and subject is not new – it has been at the heart of the human experience for millennia. The transpersonal dimension of consciousness has been known for millennia amongst various traditions, regardless of the fact that it has largely been denied and dismissed by our rational sciences. Historically, those persons more able to access this capacity – such as shamans, mystics or prophets – have often done so for the benefit of their communities.

For those who are accustomed to connecting and communicating with such realms, the notion of living, intelligent and conscious multiverses is second nature. Furthermore, virtually all human beings have the capacity to access these alternate realities. In fact, many people are already doing so without actually realizing it – casting it off as coincidence, fluke, good luck or weird anomaly. In recent years, however, there has been a significant increase in the number of people either experimenting with or experiencing what we have termed 'extra-sensory' states. These occurrences, rather than being anomalies, may well be the first wave of experiences/effects that are part of the incoming *normalization* of human perception. In other words, the 'actual experience that extra-sensory states exist may be the foundation for a future which contains extra-sensory experience as a widespread attribute'.[8] These initial experiences by the few early on are part of the natural process of acclimatizing the human being to a reality/state so that these realities can become actualized and normalized later.

The arrival of the Phoenix Generation and the resulting renaissance will stimulate the acceptance that humanity currently lives/perceives within a three-dimensional reality but in actuality exists within a multilayered web of many-dimensional realities. In this way those of the Phoenix Generation will be here to help usher in the normalizing of the multiverse. As a sentient species, humanity on Earth will be allowed to grow up one more crucial step.

New Dimensional Perspectives

Consciousness researcher Dr Rick Strassman believes that communication with transpersonal realms of experience may help humanity along its own evolution, as well as with the problems we are currently facing here on Earth:

> Establishing – with a sober, altruistic intent – reliable and generally available means of contact with these different levels of existence may help us alleviate some of the pressing issues we are facing on this planet in this time–space continuum. It even may be that the information and resources we gather in these noncorporeal realms are more important to our survival – and ultimately our evolution – than that which we obtain via strictly physical means.[9]

The idea of contact with 'non-corporeal' realms having a function in our evolution offers a new perspective upon the path – and role – of human life. Not only have non-corporeal realms of consciousness been known for millennia amongst various traditions, but also the occurrence of communication and interaction with other non-human intelligences has been widely known across human cultures.

In recent history one aspect of this communion that has attracted particular and controversial attention has been the phenomenon known as alien abduction. Despite the temptation to offer an initial reaction of either dismissal and/or anxiety, it may be that other aspects are involved in some of these experiences: elements of the transpersonal or the transformative. John E Mack, a professor of psychiatry at Harvard Medical School, in his later years became a leading authority on the spiritual or transformational effects of the alien-abduction experience. Mack came to view the alien-abduction phenomenon as acting as a catalyst to 'shatter the boundaries of the psyche and to open consciousness to a wider sense of existence and connection in the universe'.[10]

For more than a decade Mack rigorously studied the alien-abduction phenomenon and interviewed hundreds of 'abductees' (whom Mack referred to as 'experiencers'). What initially started out as an exercise in studying mental illness soon turned into an in-depth inquiry into personal and spiritual transformation. Mack eventually came to see the alien-abduction phenomenon as one of the most powerful agents for spiritual growth, personal transformation and expanded awareness. Despite the external anxiety produced by the experience, it was clear to both Mack and his set of experiencers that a profound communion was being established between humankind and other realities. Further, he concluded that this interaction was catalyzing a shift in human consciousness toward collapsing the old models of materialistic duality and opening up a connection not only 'beyond the Earth' but with other dimensional realities. Mack noted that, 'The process of psychospiritual opening that the abduction phenomenon provokes may bring experiencers to a still deeper level of consciousness where the oneness or interconnectedness of creation becomes a compelling reality.'[11]

This interconnectedness became a channel for the experiencers to receive an impressive range of information on subjects such as healing knowledge, spiritual truths, science, technology and ecology. A major part of the information apparently concerns the status of the Earth and humanity's relationship with its environment. Many of the subjects referred to their own abduction experience as participating in a transdimensional or interspecies relationship. Significantly, the transformative effects of these unusual encounters were often remarkable.

Mack's experiencers talked about an expansion of psychic or intuitive abilities; a heightened reverence for nature; the feeling of having a special mission on Earth; the collapse of space/time perception; an understanding of the multiple dimensions of reality and the existence of multiverses; a feeling of connection with all of creation; and a whole range of related transpersonal experiences. Significant from these accounts is that, according to the experiencers, the abduction phenomenon is sometimes accompanied by a sense of moving into, or connecting with, other realities or dimensions. One of the experiencers (known as 'Greg') said that, 'I think one way that the world is going to pull itself out of the problems is to let in the other realm,'[12] saying further that there was the sense as if a veil is being broken down and realities are merging – or rather another dimensional reality is being allowed into ours.

'Jean' came to the self-understanding that she was 'one of a number of people who were being neurologically reprogrammed to be transceivers', whilst 'Carol' believes 'we have been shifted or changed in some form. Not just *some* form, a vibratory form, a vibratory way. It is like we're accelerating.'[13] These comments on the alien-abduction experience are revealing as they speak about catalyzing self-development and evolutionary growth.

Important is the idea that some experiencers feel they have become 'transceivers' of a vibratory form/level. It is as if these abductees were part of a larger project of stimulating evolutionary growth within humanity by altering their vibratory frequency and placing them back into society. Many of the experiencers had a feeling that they were being reprogrammed at a cellular level so that they would be able to receive the 'vibratory information' necessary in order to disseminate it for others. According to Mack's research, experiencers spoke about encountering a vibration that filled all their cells. This was necessary, according to the experiencers' intuition, in order to raise their vibratory level to attune them to the vibrations of the beings in the alien encounter, as well as to the 'universal energy fields'. On some occasions the heightened vibratory state allowed the experiencers to communicate telepathically with the other beings or to connect with a different dimension of reality. Several reports spoke about the heightened bodily vibration being linked to a sense of awakening consciousness at a cellular level. Consequently, many of the experiencers felt they had undergone some sort of permanent change in the vibratory frequency of their bodies as a result of their abduction experiences.[14]

In this context I am not saying that all alien-abduction cases have similar origins, or that all are valid accounts of a transpersonal nature. Neither am I rushing to certify that all alien-abduction accounts give credence to the view that actual physical entities are entering into our airspace by means of some vehicle or craft. What I do wish to propose here is that there appears to be a significant number of non-ordinary consciousness states being activated – through the 'alien-abduction medium' – that may be acting as evolutionary catalysts in the broadening of the human perceptual faculty.

John Mack's research into the in-depth experience of the alien-abduction phenomenon relates to what was discussed in earlier chapters about new generations of humanity having a different energy state and vibratory resonance with the quantum field. What I sense has been happening through a variety of socio-cultural phenomena and anomalies – drug experimentation, transpersonal states, mystery schools, out-of-body practices, alien abduction, and more – is the preparation of humanity for its next phase of evolutionary development. These earlier stages used individuals as channels – or transceivers – by which to affect the energetic/vibratory state of collective humanity. Whether we have been aware of it or not, we have been engaging in various ways in the evolutionary transformation of the human species. Furthermore, part of this transformation involves the creation of novel organs of perception with which to perceive aspects of a new, emerging reality: a reality that is multidimensional. In other words, we have been working towards normalizing the multiverse, and thus assisting in bringing it into being within the perceptual faculties of the human species. In modern vocabulary, we are beginning to download the bigger picture.

As mentioned previously, the idea that we live in a multidimensional universe populated by other intelligences and life-forms is not new to many non-Western, non-orthodox traditions and to the indigenous peoples of the world. Yet the means of access, the discipline to train the body and mind to be able to sustain this communion, have been available in past times to relatively few. Now all that is changing. The next step, it seems to me, is a major planetary roll-out – a *massification* of the evolutionary process. This is why I have spent the last few pages detailing some of the effects of the alien-abduction phenomenon. The reported result of a closer connection (in terms of understanding and vibratory state) with multiple realities and dimensions is a capacity of perception that is currently unfolding within humanity at an accelerated pace. Further, the Phoenix Generation will be amongst the first wave to emerge as part of this mass unfolding. Yet there will be no 'Big Bang' or euphoric eureka moment! Despite the evolutionary quickening inherent in this process, it will emerge as if naturally and organically within each new human generation. Those of the Phoenix Generation will be the real system-busters. Not only will they bring in new ways of doing things, with dynamic innovative energy, they will also be manifesting (and thus unfolding within humankind) a new perception of reality.

Recalibrating Reality

The capacity to access non-ordinary states of consciousness is the natural heritage of humankind. Yet the potential to do so, on a physiological level, has to be refined so that biologically speaking we are able to sustain the energies related to heightened perceptions. According to consciousness researcher Gopi Krishna, humanity

> . . . will be brought in touch with another level of creation, other intelligences and states of being pervading the universe, a universe now completely shut out from our sight because of the limited capacity of our brains.[15]

The human species may thus be on the verge of breaking free from its perceptual quarantine. The instinctual intelligence and energetic resonance of our new younger generations will see them form the initial wave (the so-called 'early adopters') of this sacred technology. They will come to recognize – as if second nature – that humanity shares a cosmic neighbourhood with a radiant profusion of other intelligences. We were never alone – and we will laugh at our old thinking for ever considering it so! We will come to consider our pre-multidimensional perspective as that of living in Flatland – a 'dimensionally flat' world where we were incapable of perceiving the expanded dimensionality that exists all around us.[16] Back in the early days of silent movies or black and white television, people knew that the reality existed in sound and colour yet they didn't have equipment capable of receiving the 'bigger picture.' Through the new generations coming into the world we will be introducing the new 'human transceiver' into the collective blueprint of the human species.

Our latest scientific discoveries are revealing to us that multidimensional energy has always been present within the innermost core of the human body. As was discussed in Chapter 9, biophoton-emitting DNA produces a field-organizing effect that overlaps, forming what is called inductance. This then amplifies the signal through creating biological coherence – what I referred to in Chapter 6 as quantum coherence. This state of coherence allows for instant communication to occur as a nonlocal energy field as each of the 100 trillion molecules in the human body emits its own magnetic field, each one over-lapping with the next one. With trillions of overlapping DNA fields – each with a mini electromagnetic field – a unified quantum state is created that could have multidimensional properties. It is known that there are magnetic fields at the centre of atomic structure that physicists refer to as interdimensional fields. Physicists are also debating whether interdimensional energy exists at the centres of galaxies, and whether galactic centres are in a quantum state. This relates to the information Ken Carey received:

> . . . the fully activated human sensory system is more than just an interdimensional communication device. In miniature it replicates in the structural pattern of its biogravitational field the same pattern found in planetary, solar, galactic, and universal fields.[17]

Our old human consciousness was not suitably prepared for accessing/receiving multidimensional experiences. However, the new energy/consciousness that will be unfolding upon this planet, and through our coming generations, will be conducive to perceiving multidimensional realities.

Those of the coming generations will understand – and act – in ways that we would never have expected, or can expect. This new understanding of being an evolving part of an intelligence-rich multidimensional existence will be humanity's shared inheritance, and not the preserve of a few. Let me stress that this is not some fantastical 'new age/golden age' hippy story – it is the natural unfolding of a different state of consciousness. In this transition to what I have termed a quantum renaissance, humanity is further 'growing up'. What this means is that as a species we will be creatively working, step by step, toward forming a planetary society that celebrates diversity within unity. We will be moving from a time when we thought we were 'alone' in a dead universe to the understanding that we are part of a vast, inconceivably rich, living 'universe within multiverses' teeming with intelligent life. Further, the capacity to perceive the existence of other-dimensional realities will be unfolding within humanity. In other words, we are moving into a time of verifiable contact with multiple forms of intelligent life. We will be joining the neighbourhood of cosmic *L.I.F.E.* – where we shall be *L*iving a more *I*ntegrated and *F*ulfilling *E*xistence. This will be the beginning of living in resonance with a new sacred reality:

> . . . all creatures inhabit and live within a single field of shared consciousness, that all are projections of a single Being, and that all of us – angels, humans, animals, vegetables, microbes and minerals – are differentiated aspects of one conscious and coherent whole. This recognition is the cornerstone of the new Sacred Reality . . .[18]

When this new perception of life – planetary, cosmic and dimensional – is integrated and normalized in the psyche of humanity, far-reaching and revolutionary change will occur in every sphere of human life.

The emergence of a more attuned instinctual intelligence will naturally foster a new form of spirituality – one that is not based upon human institutions. Instead, it will form around a sacred connection with all forms of life and with a living cosmos. It will recognize the evolutionary impulse in humankind – as a biological inheritance and process – and will nurture self-development and well-being. Human attention and energy will be diverted from the old ways of materialism ('matter realism') toward human dignity, compassion, tolerance, unity and the actualization of our togetherness. New resources will be discovered and through the energy of collaboration a new planetary society will be co-created. A process of profound transformation will occur on planet Earth as the impulse of love will nurture our collective spirit and collective intention to make a future for humanity within the cosmos.

The phoenix will have arisen from the ashes of the old consciousness and with radiant energy bring forth a new era for humanity.

The Future is a World for Us All

Or we may find when all the rest has failed
Hid in ourselves the key of perfect change.
  Sri Aurobindo, Savitri

We are the 'perfect change' that Aurobindo talks about. We are the agents of change within a physical world; change begins with us – in *matter* and in *life*. The work is a living work, a real, tangible, human experience. It is up to us to become the change that then impacts on and influences our physical surroundings. In short, we *must live it*. Satprem echoed this sentiment when he wrote

> The difficulty lies not in discovering hidden secrets, but in discovering the visible, and that unsuspected gold in the midst of all the banality . . . Unless our natural grows truer, no supernatural will ever be able to remedy it; if our inner dwelling is ugly, no miraculous crystal will brighten our days, no fruit will ever quench our thirst. Paradise must be made on Earth, or else it will be nowhere . . . It is in the body and in the daily life that we

> have to work out the transmutation, otherwise no
> gold will ever glitter, here or elsewhere, and for
> all time to come.[1]

The transmutation, as Satprem so rightly points out, is within us; and the gold that will glitter will be here on Earth. Humanity is the membrane – the physical tapestry – that weaves the fabric of consciousness and conscious forces within our reality. Knowing this must surely change not only how we perceive the world and reality around us but more importantly how we act within it.

We are neither an accident of life, nor an anomaly of life either. We are an expression of the ongoing evolutionary drama unfolding upon countless planes, multiverses and multiple dimensions. We are a family within endless spirals of families, all potentially entwined with one another just as the oceans are connected with each wave – no matter how far away it crests and falls, and regardless of which shore the wave crashes against and dampens. Boundaries are the illusions of a sleeping consciousness, the dreams of a soul not yet bloomed into being.

Our quarantine is soon to be lifted, and humanity as a species will be thrust forward not only toward the creation of a planetary society here on Earth but also into an age of cosmic humanism. We must be prepared to live consciously all the capacities we have dwelling within us unconsciously. We must also bring forth and nurture our human energies in unity. This means balancing our masculine and feminine values, nurturing a harmony that is collaborative and not competitive. The energies of dominance and rivalry will not survive into the future – neither in our human institutions nor within each of us. We must unfold and manifest the energies that bring together, not those that tear apart: energies that unify and not divide. We must respect the role of the female in all our societies, and nurture the caring energies within each of us, including men. The future is a world for all of us – and together, with our new young arrivals, we can make it a blessed future.

Notes and References

Introduction

1. As was evidenced by the 2012 hype.
2. See *New Revolutions for a Small Planet* and *New Consciousness for a New World*.
3. See my previous books, *Breaking the Spell* and *The Struggle For Your Mind*.

Chapter 1

1. The growth of complex systems can lead to a fragile breaking point. In this context overshoot occurs when the long-term carrying capacity of the environment is exceeded, and a tipping-point (or die-off) is triggered.

Chapter 2

1. William Irwin Thompson, *Passages About Earth: An Exploration of the New Planetary Culture*. New York: Harper & Row, 1974, pp. 119–20.
2. Richard Tarnas, 'Is the Modern Psyche Undergoing a Rite of Passage?', 2001, www.cosmosandpsyche.com/Essays.php.
3. Richard Heinberg, *Memories and Visions of Paradise: Exploring the Universal Myth of a Lost Golden Age*. Wellingborough: Aquarian Press, 1990, p. 116.
4. Idries Shah, *Special Illumination*. London: Octagon Press, 1977, p. 43.

Chapter 3

1. Tarnas, 'Is the Modern Psyche Undergoing a Rite of Passage?', p. 19.

2. Integral consciousness refers to the consciousness structures described by Jean Gebser, and refers to a new relationship to space and time and an awareness of the whole.

Chapter 4

1. P M H Atwater, *Beyond the Indigo Children: The New Children and the Coming of the Fifth World*. Rochester, VT: Bear & Co., 2005.
2. Ibid.
3. Sri Aurobindo, *The Human Cycle: The Psychology of Social Development*. Twin Lakes, WI: Lotus Light Publications, 1999 [1950], p. 71.
4. Llewellyn Vaughan-Lee, *The Return of the Feminine and the World Soul*. Point Reyes, CA: Golden Sufi Center, 2009, p. 25.

Chapter 5

1. See Henri Bergson, *Creative Evolution* (1907, in English 1911); Jan Smuts, *Holism and Evolution* (1926); and Alfred North Whitehead, *Process and Reality* (1929).
2. See www.hole-in-the-wall.com/Beginnings.html.
3. For more on these youth innovators, see http://mashable.com/2013/03/03/youth-innovators.
4. J Chilton Pearce, *Evolution's End: Claiming the Potential of Our Intelligence*. New York: HarperCollins, 1992.
5. D Siegel, *Mindsight: Transform your Brain with the New Science of Kindness*, Oneworld Publications, 2010, p. 42.
6. See www.generationwakingup.org.
7. For event schedules see http://genup.net.
8. Quote sourced from Buckminster Fuller, *Synergetics: Explorations in the Geometry of Thinking*. New York: Prentice Hall, 1975.

Chapter 6

1. Ervin László and Kingsley Dennis, *Dawn of the Akashic Age: New Consciousness, Quantum Resonance, and the Future of the World*. Rochester, VT: Inner Traditions, 2013.
2. Man-Wan Ho, *The Rainbow and the Worm: The Physics of Organisms*. Singapore: World Scientific, 1998.
3. F-A Popp, K H Li, W P Mei, M Galle and R Neurohr, 'Physical Aspects of Biophotons', *Experientia*, 1988, 44, pp. 576–85.
4. R O Becker, *The Body Electric*, 1998, William Morrow.
5. Siegel, *Mindsight*.

6. Larry Dossey, *One Mind: How Our Individual Mind Is Part of a Greater Consciousness and Why It Matters*. London: Hay House, 2013.
7. Cited in T Pfeiffer and J Mack (eds), *Mind Before Matter: Visions of a New Science of Consciousness*. Winchester: O Books, 2007, pp. 78–9.
8. In personal conversation with colleague Frithjoff Bergmann.
9. The Revolutionary Armed Forces of Colombia–People's Army (Fuerzas Armadas Revolucionarias de Colombia – Ejército del Pueblo, FARC-EP or FARC) is a Colombian Marxist-Leninist revolutionary guerrilla organization involved in the continuing Colombian armed conflict since 1964 (Wikipedia).
10. See Paul Mason's, *Why It's STILL Kicking Off Everywhere: The New Global Revolutions*. London: Verso, 2013.
11. See www.energeticxchange.com.
12. See a video of this conversation between George Kaponay and Lugas, www.youtube.com/watch?v=r_ueiSci_nY&feature=player_embedded.

Chapter 7

1. Taken from James Surowiecki, *The Wisdom of Crowds: Why the Many Are Smarter than the Few and How Collective Wisdom Shapes Business, Economies, Societies and Nations*. New York: Abacus, 2005.
2. Taken from Harrison Owen, *Wave Rider: Leadership for High Performance in a Self-Organizing World*. San Francisco, CA: Berrett-Koehler, 2008.
3. R D Steele, *The Open-Source Everything Manifesto: Transparency, Truth & Trust*. Berkeley, CA: Evolver Editions, 2012.
4. From Robert Frost, 'The Road Not Taken'.
5. R Willis, M Webb and J Wilsdon, *The Disrupters: Lessons for Low-Carbon Innovation from the New Wave of Environmental Pioneers*. London: Nesta, 2007.
6. Edward De Bono, *New Thinking for the New Millennium*. London: Penguin, 2000, p. 279.
7. See http://laptop.org/en.
8. J Rifkin, *The Third Industrial Revolution*. London: Palgrave Macmillan, 2011, p. 252.
9. Michael Nielsen, *Reinventing Discovery: The New Era of Networked Science*. Princeton, NJ: Princeton University Press, 2011.
10. László and Dennis, *Dawn of the Akashic Age*.

11. Sri Aurobindo, *The Human Cycle: The Psychology of Social Development*. Twin Lakes, WI: Lotus Light Publications, 1999 [1950], p. 263.

Chapter 8

1. Darold A. Treffert, *Extraordinary People: Understanding Savant Syndrome*.
2. P M H Atwater, *The New Children and Near-Death Experiences*. Rochester, VT: Bear & Co., 2003.
2. Atwater, p. 35.
3. The names of these individuals have been changed to protect their identities.
4. Atwater, p. 161.
5. Atwater, p. 95.
6. Kenneth Ring, *The Omega Project: Near-Death Experiences, UFO Encounters, and Mind at Large*. New York: William Morrow, 1992.
7. Margot Grey, *Return From Death: An Exploration of the Near-Death Experience*. London: Arkana, 1986.
8. Atwater, *Beyond the Indigo Children*.
9. Lee Carroll and Jan Tober, *The Indigo Children 10 Years Later*. London: Hay House, 2009.
10. Carroll & Tober, p. ix.
11. See www.youtube.com/watch?v=Bx5Sc3vWefE.
12. See my earlier book *The Struggle for Your Mind: Conscious Evolution & The Battle to Control How We Think*.

Chapter 9

1. This limitation is due to the fact that humans, as bipedals, have a narrow birth canal.
2. Also see Rupert Sheldrake's 'Morphic resonance/fields' hypothesis as outlined in *A New Science of Life* (new edition titled *Morphic Resonance: The Nature of Formative Causation*).
3. Man-Wan Ho, *The Rainbow and the Worm: The Physics of Organisms*. Singapore: World Scientific, 1998.
4. 'In electromagnetism and electronics, inductance is the property of a conductor by which a change in current in the conductor "induces" (creates) a voltage (electromotive force) in both the conductor itself (self-inductance) and in any nearby conductors (mutual inductance)' – Wikipedia.
5. See my earlier book *The Struggle for Your Mind*.
6. Idries Shah, *The Sufis*. London: Octagon, 1982, p. 54.
7. Taken from Rumi's *Mathnawi*.

8. R Bucke, *Cosmic Consciousness: A Study in the Evolution of the Human Mind.* London: Olympia Press, 1972 [1901].
9. Gopi Krishna, *Higher Consciousness and Kundalini.* Ontario, Canada: F.I.N.D. Research Trust, 1993, p. 166.
10. S E Gulbekian, *In the Belly of the Beast: Holding Your Own in Mass Culture.* Charlottesville, VA: Hampton Roads, 2004, p. 251.
11. *New Consciousness for a New World.* Rochester, VT: Inner Traditions, 2011.
12. M Blank and R Goodman, 'Do Electromagnetic Fields Interact Directly with DNA?', *Bioelectromagnetics*, 18, 1997, pp. 111–15.
13. J Narby, *Cosmic Serpent: DNA and the Origins of Knowledge.* London: Phoenix, 1999.
14. The process whereby two oscillating systems come into synchronization and share a common frequency.
15. For example the work of Paramahansa Yogananda.
16. K Carey, *The Starseed Transmissions.* New York: HarperCollins, 1995 [1982], p. 47.
17. Carey, p. 41.
18. See http://noosphere.princeton.edu.
19. Jalal ad-Din Rumi (trans. Coleman Barks), 'Two Kinds of Intelligence', *Mathnawi* IV: 1960–1968.

Chapter 10

1. Satprem, *Evolution II.* Paris: Institut des Recherches Evolutives, 1995, p. 95.
2. See Wikipedia, 'Punctuated equilibrium'.
3. Literally, as evidence shows there are correlations between solar activity and evolutionary processes: see Dieter Broers, *Solar Revolution: Why Mankind Is on the Cusp of an Evolutionary Leap.* Berkeley, CA: Evolver Editions, 2012.
4. Jose Arguelles, *Manifesto for the Noosphere: The Next Stage in the Evolution of Human Consciousness.* Berkeley, CA: Evolver Editions, 2011, cited on p. 27.
5. László and Dennis, *Dawn of the Akashic Age.*
6. From William Shakespeare's *As You Like It* (Act II, Scene VII).
7. Jacky Law, *Big Pharma: How the World's Biggest Drug Companies Control Illness.* London: Robinson Publishing, 2006; Ben Goldacre, *Bad Pharma: How Drug Companies Mislead Doctors and Harm Patients.* London: Fourth Estate, 2012.
8. Larry Dossey, *Reinventing Medicine: Beyond Mind-Body to a New Era of Healing.* New York: HarperCollins, 1999.
9. Dossey, p. 115.
10. Adam, *Complete Dreamhealer.* London: Piatkus, 2009, p. 174.
11. Adam, *Complete Dreamhealer.*

Chapter 11

1. This is known as cymatics – see Wikipedia, 'Cymatics'.
2. Cited in Pfeiffer and Mack, *Mind Before Matter*, p. 96.
3. Estimates of the number of major mass extinctions in the last 540 million years range from as few as five to more than twenty (wikipedia.org 'Extinction event').
4. Doris Lessing, *Prisons We Choose To Live Inside*. London: HarperCollins, 1987, p. 6.
5. See Wikipedia, 'Panspermia'.
6. Francis Crick, *Life Itself: Its Origin and Nature*. New York: Simon & Schuster, 1981.
7. Ervin László, *The Self-Actualizing Cosmos: The Akasha Revolution in Science*. Rochester, VT: Inner Traditions, 2014.
8. Ernest Scott, *The People of the Secret*. London: Octagon Press, 1985, p. 237.
9. R Strassman et al., *Inner Paths to Outer Space: Journeys to Alien Worlds through Psychedelics and Other Spiritual Technologies*. Rochester, VT: Park Street Press, 2008, p. 80.
10. John E Mack, *Passport to the Cosmos: Human Transformation & Alien Encounters,* New York, Crown Publishers, 1999, p. 218.
11. Mack, p. 136.
12. Mack, p. 61.
13. Interestingly, one of the experiencers was shown a vision of a phoenix which, for him, symbolized 'the species of aliens from all parts of the galaxy and perhaps other dimensions'. This same experiencer further remarked that the phoenix symbol is 'so deep, it is universal in nature' – this information was unknown to me when I developed the concept of the Phoenix Generation and decided upon the title of this book.
14. Mack, p. 78.
15. Krishna, *Higher Consciousness and Kundalini*, p. 197.
16. A reference to *Flatland: A Romance of Many Dimensions*, an 1884 satirical novella by Edwin A Abbott about a two-dimensional world, referred to as 'Flatland', which is occupied by geometric figures.
17. Ken Carey, *The Third Millennium: Living in the Posthistoric World,* New York, HarperCollins, 1996, p. 94.
18. Ken Carey, *Return of the Bird Tribes*. New York: HarperCollins, 1988, p. 169.

Epilogue

1. Satprem, *On the Way to Supermanhood*. Mysore, India: Mira Aditi, 2002 [1974], pp. 83–4.

Bibliography

Adam, *Complete Dreamhealer*. London: Piatkus, 2009

Arguelles, Jose, *Manifesto for the Noosphere: The Next Stage in the Evolution of Human Consciousness*. Berkeley, CA: Evolver Editions, 2011

Atwater, P M H, *The New Children and Near-Death Experiences*. Rochester, VT: Bear & Co., 2003

——, *Beyond the Indigo Children: The New Children and the Coming of the Fifth World*. Rochester, VT: Bear & Co., 2005

Aurobindo, Sri, *The Human Cycle: The Psychology of Social Development*. Twin Lakes, WI: Lotus Light Publications, 1999 [1950]

Becker, Robert O, *The Body Electric*. New York: William Morrow, 1998

Bucke, R, *Cosmic Consciousness: A Study in the Evolution of the Human Mind*. London: The Olympia Press, 1972 [1901]

Carey, Ken, *The Starseed Transmissions*. New York: HarperCollins, 1995 [1982]

——, *Return of the Bird Tribes*. New York: HarperCollins, 1988

Carey, Ken, *The Third Millennium: Living in the Posthistoric World*. New York: HarperCollins, 1996

Carroll, Lee, & Jan Tober, *The Indigo Children: The New Kids Have Arrived*. London: Hay House, 1999

——, *The Indigo Children 10 Years Later*. London: Hay House, 2009

Chilton Pearce, J, *Evolution's End: Claiming the Potential of Our Intelligence*. New York: HarperCollins, 1992

Crick, Francis, *Life Itself: Its Origin and Nature*. New York: Simon & Schuster, 1981

De Bono, Edward, *New Thinking for the New Millennium*. London: Penguin, 2000

Dennis, Kingsley L, *New Consciousness for a New World*. Rochester: VT: Inner Traditions, 2011

——, *The Struggle for Your Mind*. Rochester: VT: Inner Traditions, 2012

——, *New Revolutions for a Small Planet*. London: Watkins Books, 2012

——, *Breaking the Spell: An Exploration of Human Perception*. Winchester: O Books, 2013

Dossey, Larry, *Reinventing Medicine: Beyond Mind-Body to a New Era of Healing*. New York: HarperCollins, 1999

Goldacre, Ben, *Bad Pharma: How Drug Companies Mislead Doctors and Harm Patients*. London: Fourth Estate, 2012

Grey, Margot, *Return From Death: An Exploration of the Near-Death Experience*. London: Arkana, 1986

Gulbekian, S E, *In the Belly of the Beast: Holding Your Own in Mass Culture*. Charlottesville, VA: Hampton Roads, 2004

Ho, Man-Wan, *The Rainbow and the Worm: The Physics of Organisms*. Singapore: World Scientific, 1998

Krishna, Gopi, *Higher Consciousness and Kundalini*. Ontario, Canada: F.I.N.D. Research Trust, 1993

László, Ervin, & Kingsley Dennis, *Dawn of the Akashic Age: New Consciousness, Quantum Resonance, and the Future of the World*. Rochester: VT: Inner Traditions, 2013

Law, Jacky, *Big Pharma: How the World's Biggest Drug Companies Control Illness*. London: Robinson Publishing, 2006

Lessing, Doris, *Shikasta*. New York: Alfred A. Knopf, 1979

——, *Prisons We Choose To Live Inside*. London: HarperCollins, 1987

Mack, John, E, *Passport to the Cosmos: Human Transformation & Alien Encounters*. New York: Crown Publishers, 1999

Mason, Paul, *Why It's STILL Kicking Off Everywhere: The New Global Revolutions*. London: Verso, 1999

Narby, J, *Cosmic Serpent: DNA and the Origins of Knowledge*. London: Phoenix, 1999

Nielsen, Michael, *Reinventing Discovery: The New Era of Networked Science*. Princeton, NJ: Princeton University Press, 2011

Pfeiffer, T, & J E Mack (eds), *Mind Before Matter: Visions of a New Science of Consciousness*. Winchester: O Books, 2007

Rifkin, Jeremy, *The Third Industrial Revolution*. London: Palgrave Macmillan, 2011

Ring, Kenneth, *The Omega Project: Near-Death Experiences, UFO Encounters, and Mind at Large*. New York: William Morrow, 1992

Rumi, Jalal ad-Din (trans. Coleman Barks), *Mathnawi*. Gibb Memorial Trust, 2001 [1926]

Satprem, *On the Way to Supermanhood*. Mysore, India: Mira Aditi, 2002 [1974]

——, *Evolution II*. Paris: Institut des Recherches Evolutives, 1995

Scott, Ernest, *The People of the Secret*. London: Octagon Press, 1985

Shah, Idries, *Special Illumination*. London: Octagon Press, 1977

——, *The Sufis*. London: Octagon, 1982

Siegel, Daniel, *Mindsight: Transform you Brain with the New Science of Kindness*. Oxford: Oneworld Publications, 2010

Steele, Robert D, *The Open-Source Everything Manifesto: Transparency, Truth & Trust*. Berkeley, CA: Evolver Editions, 2012

Strassman, R., S Wojtowicz, L Eduardo Luna, & E Frecska, *Inner Paths to Outer Space: Journeys to Alien Worlds through Psychedelics and Other Spiritual Technologies*. Rochester, VT: Park Street Press, 2008

Willis, R, M Webb, & J Wilsdon, *The Disrupters: Lessons for Low-Carbon Innovation from the New Wave of Environmental Pioneers*. London: Nesta, 2007

Acknowledgements

With many thanks to John Tintera, whose enthusiasm for the book was much appreciated right from the start. It was a delight travelling the publishing path with John, whose mixture of humour and savvy has been a breath of fresh air!

My thanks to Michael Mann, whose keen support once again achieved another successful project. Thumbs up!

Also, my thanks to Donald Sommerville whose professional copy-editing managed to rid the book of those odd grammatical errors that always seem to creep in when the author is unawares – you did a grand job!

Finally, thank you to everyone at Watkins Publishing for nurturing the book into the world.

In gratitude & appreciation.

Index

abundance model 31–2
ADD (attention-deficit disorder)
  51
ADHD (attention-deficit
  hyperactivity disorder) 51
Akashic Age 93, 175–6
alien abduction phenomenon
  215–18
American Transcendentalism
  70–1
Apollo space programme 90
Arab Spring 102
ASD (autistic spectrum disorder)
  51–2
AS (Asperger syndrome) 51
Atwater, P M H 133–4, 135, 137
Aurobindo, Sri 4, 53, 67, 122–3,
  127, 225
Autobiography of a Yogi 70

babies: comparison of human
  to baby animals 148–9;
  instinctual intelligence of 149;
  size of heads 147–8
Bailey, Alice 69
Ball, Zora 82
Besant, Annie 69
Bioelectromagnetics 159–60

biological coherence 93–4, 95
biophysics 93–4
biotechnology 196
Blavatsky, Helena 69
blotting paper analogy 35–6
Bridge Generation:
  ambassadorial responsibilities
  36–7; the 'calling' 59–63;
  collective consciousness
  17, 54, 98, 155; connecting
  people through networks
  74–5; current generation 6;
  decreasing physical resources
  and finances 51; diffusion of
  knowledge and information
  54; frustration at slow pace
  of change 35; generational
  change 61; importance
  of sincerity 55; living
  work 55–9; new forms of
  spirituality 62–3; nourishing
  the finer impacts 32–3;
  resources for development
  and empowerment 37;
  responsibility for children
  51–3; responsibility for
  constructive change 40;
  self-realization of people 63;

physical transmutation 31;
psychological consciousness
69, 72; resisting 'fear of
freedom' 5; rewiring of
thinking and behaviour
patterns 75, 83–4; self-
actualization 62; spiritualism
and 69–73; transformation
of 73–4; unbalanced self 15;
unconscious mind 30–1; *see
also* human life; psyche
psychoanalysis 71, 72
public spaces 14–15

quantum coherence 93, 94, 150,
152, 162, 163
quantum communication 195
quantum computing 195
quantum consciousness 153
quantum DNA 150–1, 152, 157
quantum instinct and
intelligence 149
quantum physics 71–2, 91–2
quantum renaissance:
emergence of planetary
human 172; new era 6; new
models of understanding
174–5; newer seed energy
173, 175; quantum whole
175; recalibrations *see*
recalibrations

recalibrations: cosmic awareness
204–6, 207–8, 209; education
and learning 185–8; emerging
technologies 194–6; health
180–5; human spirit and
wisdom 177–80; media
and lifestyle 188–91; new
economics 191–3; new
energies 199–203; politics
196–9
relationships, operating at a
distance 100

Renaissance of Replacement:
distributed networks 76;
emerging innovations and
new models 2; smooth social
transition 2–3, 26
resonance *see* fields of resonance
resources, struggle for control
of 18
rhetoric 42–3
Rifkin, Jeremy 117
Ring, Kenneth 135, 135–6
Ritalin 52
Rumi, Jalal ad-Din 5–6, 59, 151,
169

sacred reality 223
salat 167–8
Satprem 171, 172, 225–6
savants 131–2
science: collaboration between
amateurs and scientists 118;
networked science 118; reflection of spiritual growth 120
self-awareness 85–6
*The sentimental agents in the
Volyen Empire* 42
Shah, Idries 151
shamanic practices 160
SID (sensory-integration
dysfunction) 51
Siegel, Daniel 84, 85, 94–5
social agents of change 41
social history, neglect of
psychological understanding 3
social networks, empathy and
sharing intimacy 76–8
social order, grisly elf 3–4
social systems: diminution of
central hierarchy 130–1;
exposition of corruption and
wrongdoing 141–2; facade
of rulers 144; increased
transparency in 141;
obsolescence of 157; seeds of

integrity 175
solar radiation 159
sound/vibration waves 208–9
soundbites 16
space: quantum field of 92;
    reality of 91–2
spiritualism 62–3, 69–73
stars 212
Steele, Robert David 108
Steiner, Krishnamurti and Rudolf
    69
Strassman, Dr Rick 214
swine flu 180
synaesthesia 134, 138

Tappe, Nancy Ann 138–9, 139
Tarnas, Richard 30–1, 40
technologies: biotechnology
    and 196; cloud space
    194; communication
    and collaboration 194;
    connectivity 194, 195;
    innovations in 101; quantum
    computing 195
teleportation 91–2
Theosophical Society 69
theosophy 69
Thompson, William Irwin 27–9
Toynbee, Arnold 40–1
truth, nature of 42

Un Millón de Voces Contra Las
    FARC 102–3
universe *see* multiverses

vaccinations controversies 180–1
Vaughan-Lee, Llewellyn 61
vocabulary 25

well-being: illusion of 16; true
    richness of 14–15

William (NDE subject) 134
wisdom *see* human spirit
witches 55
world systems 45

Yogananda, Paramahansa 70
young generation: awareness
    about health issues 181;
    citizens of the world 176;
    common sense flow 142–3;
    community and social
    project involvement 79;
    creative intelligence of 157;
    desensitized to extreme
    violence 52–3; dialogue of
    peace and reconciliation 87–9;
    education and learning 185–8;
    empathetic consciousness
    82–3; empathy and sharing
    intimacy 97; innate computer
    skills 80–1; inner knowing
    162; innovative change and
    81–2; intentional coherence
    168–9; Internet creativity 80;
    lifestyle 190–1; limitations
    of belief systems 142;
    mental illness and disorder
    51–2; networks of friends
    76; prescription drug usage
    52; questioning authority
    139–40, 141–2; resistance to
    old-model thinking 176–7;
    self-initiated awakening
    162; sense of purpose 179;
    transformational change 143;
    see also childhood; children;
    instinctual intelligence; media;
    NDEs